HENRY VI, PART 2

WILLIAM SHAKESPEARE

Dramatis Personae

KING HENRY THE SIXTH
HUMPHREY, DUKE OF GLOUCESTER, his uncle
CARDINAL BEAUFORT, BISHOP OF WINCHESTER, great-uncle to the King
RICHARD PLANTAGENET, DUKE OF YORK
EDWARD and RICHARD, his sons
DUKE OF SOMERSET
DUKE OF SUFFOLK
DUKE OF BUCKINGHAM
LORD CLIFFORD
YOUNG CLIFFORD, his son
EARL OF SALISBURY
EARL OF WARWICK
LORD SCALES
LORD SAY
SIR HUMPHREY STAFFORD
WILLIAM STAFFORD, his brother
SIR JOHN STANLEY
VAUX
MATTHEW GOFFE
A LIEUTENANT, a SHIPMASTER, a MASTER'S MATE, and WALTER WHITMORE
TWO GENTLEMEN, prisoners with Suffolk
JOHN HUME and JOHN SOUTHWELL, two priests
ROGER BOLINGBROKE, a conjurer
A SPIRIT raised by him
THOMAS HORNER, an armourer
PETER, his man
CLERK OF CHATHAM
MAYOR OF SAINT ALBANS
SAUNDER SIMPCOX, an impostor
ALEXANDER IDEN, a Kentish gentleman
JACK CADE, a rebel

5

GEORGE BEVIS, JOHN HOLLAND, DICK THE BUTCHER,
SMITH THE WEAVER,
  MICHAEL, &c., followers of Cade
TWO MURDERERS

MARGARET, Queen to King Henry
ELEANOR, Duchess of Gloucester
MARGERY JOURDAIN, a witch
WIFE to SIMPCOX

Lords, Ladies, and Attendants; Petitioners, Aldermen, a Herald,
  a Beadle, a Sheriff, Officers, Citizens, Prentices, Falconers,
  Guards, Soldiers, Messengers, &c.

SCENE: England

ACT I. SCENE I. London. The palace

Flourish of trumpets; then hautboys. Enter the KING, DUKE
HUMPHREY OF GLOUCESTER, SALISBURY, WARWICK, and
CARDINAL BEAUFORT, on the one side; the QUEEN,
SUFFOLK, YORK, SOMERSET, and BUCKINGHAM, on the
other

  SUFFOLK. As by your high imperial Majesty
    I had in charge at my depart for France,
    As procurator to your Excellence,
    To marry Princess Margaret for your Grace;
    So, in the famous ancient city Tours,
    In presence of the Kings of France and Sicil,
    The Dukes of Orleans, Calaber, Bretagne, and Alencon,
    Seven earls, twelve barons, and twenty reverend bishops,
    I have perform'd my task, and was espous'd;
    And humbly now upon my bended knee,
    In sight of England and her lordly peers,
    Deliver up my title in the Queen
    To your most gracious hands, that are the substance
    Of that great shadow I did represent:
    The happiest gift that ever marquis gave,
    The fairest queen that ever king receiv'd.
  KING HENRY. Suffolk, arise. Welcome, Queen Margaret:
    I can express no kinder sign of love
    Than this kind kiss. O Lord, that lends me life,
    Lend me a heart replete with thankfulness!
    For thou hast given me in this beauteous face
    A world of earthly blessings to my soul,
    If sympathy of love unite our thoughts.

QUEEN. Great King of England, and my gracious lord,
  The mutual conference that my mind hath had,
  By day, by night, waking and in my dreams,
  In courtly company or at my beads,
  With you, mine alder-liefest sovereign,
  Makes me the bolder to salute my king
  With ruder terms, such as my wit affords
  And over-joy of heart doth minister.
KING HENRY. Her sight did ravish, but her grace in speech,
  Her words y-clad with wisdom's majesty,
  Makes me from wond'ring fall to weeping joys,
  Such is the fulness of my heart's content.
  Lords, with one cheerful voice welcome my love.
ALL. [Kneeling] Long live Queen Margaret, England's happiness!
QUEEN. We thank you all. [Flourish]
SUFFOLK. My Lord Protector, so it please your Grace,
  Here are the articles of contracted peace
  Between our sovereign and the French King Charles,
  For eighteen months concluded by consent.
GLOUCESTER. [Reads] 'Imprimis: It is agreed between the
French King
  Charles and William de la Pole, Marquess of Suffolk, ambassador
  for Henry King of England, that the said Henry shall espouse the
  Lady Margaret, daughter unto Reignier King of Naples, Sicilia,
  and Jerusalem, and crown her Queen of England ere the thirtieth
  of May next ensuing.
    Item: That the duchy of Anjou and the county of Maine shall be
  released and delivered to the King her father'-
                      [Lets the paper fall]
KING HENRY. Uncle, how now!
GLOUCESTER. Pardon me, gracious lord;
  Some sudden qualm hath struck me at the heart,
  And dimm'd mine eyes, that I can read no further.
KING HENRY. Uncle of Winchester, I pray read on.
CARDINAL. [Reads] 'Item: It is further agreed between them that
the
  duchies of Anjou and Maine shall be released and delivered over
  to the King her father, and she sent over of the King of
  England's own proper cost and charges, without having any

8

dowry.'

KING HENRY. They please us well. Lord Marquess, kneel down.
We here create thee the first Duke of Suffolk,
And girt thee with the sword. Cousin of York,
We here discharge your Grace from being Regent
I' th' parts of France, till term of eighteen months
Be full expir'd. Thanks, uncle Winchester,
Gloucester, York, Buckingham, Somerset,
Salisbury, and Warwick;
We thank you all for this great favour done
In entertainment to my princely queen.
Come, let us in, and with all speed provide
To see her coronation be perform'd.
                    Exeunt KING, QUEEN, and SUFFOLK
GLOUCESTER. Brave peers of England, pillars of the state,
To you Duke Humphrey must unload his grief
Your grief, the common grief of all the land.
What! did my brother Henry spend his youth,
His valour, coin, and people, in the wars?
Did he so often lodge in open field,
In winter's cold and summer's parching heat,
To conquer France, his true inheritance?
And did my brother Bedford toil his wits
To keep by policy what Henry got?
Have you yourselves, Somerset, Buckingham,
Brave York, Salisbury, and victorious Warwick,
Receiv'd deep scars in France and Normandy?
Or hath mine uncle Beaufort and myself,
With all the learned Council of the realm,
Studied so long, sat in the Council House
Early and late, debating to and fro
How France and Frenchmen might be kept in awe?
And had his Highness in his infancy
Crowned in Paris, in despite of foes?
And shall these labours and these honours die?
Shall Henry's conquest, Bedford's vigilance,
Your deeds of war, and all our counsel die?
O peers of England, shameful is this league!
Fatal this marriage, cancelling your fame,

Blotting your names from books of memory,
Razing the characters of your renown,
Defacing monuments of conquer'd France,
Undoing all, as all had never been!
CARDINAL. Nephew, what means this passionate discourse,
This peroration with such circumstance?
For France, 'tis ours; and we will keep it still.
GLOUCESTER. Ay, uncle, we will keep it if we can;
But now it is impossible we should.
Suffolk, the new-made duke that rules the roast,
Hath given the duchy of Anjou and Maine
Unto the poor King Reignier, whose large style
Agrees not with the leanness of his purse.
SALISBURY. Now, by the death of Him that died for all,
These counties were the keys of Normandy!
But wherefore weeps Warwick, my valiant son?
WARWICK. For grief that they are past recovery;
For were there hope to conquer them again
My sword should shed hot blood, mine eyes no tears.
Anjou and Maine! myself did win them both;
Those provinces these arms of mine did conquer;
And are the cities that I got with wounds
Deliver'd up again with peaceful words?
Mort Dieu!
YORK. For Suffolk's duke, may he be suffocate,
That dims the honour of this warlike isle!
France should have torn and rent my very heart
Before I would have yielded to this league.
I never read but England's kings have had
Large sums of gold and dowries with their wives;
And our King Henry gives away his own
To match with her that brings no vantages.
GLOUCESTER. A proper jest, and never heard before,
That Suffolk should demand a whole fifteenth
For costs and charges in transporting her!
She should have stay'd in France, and starv'd in France,
Before-
CARDINAL. My Lord of Gloucester, now ye grow too hot:
It was the pleasure of my lord the King.

10

GLOUCESTER. My Lord of Winchester, I know your mind;
'Tis not my speeches that you do mislike,
But 'tis my presence that doth trouble ye.
Rancour will out: proud prelate, in thy face
I see thy fury; if I longer stay
We shall begin our ancient bickerings.
Lordings, farewell; and say, when I am gone,
I prophesied France will be lost ere long. Exit
CARDINAL. So, there goes our Protector in a rage.
'Tis known to you he is mine enemy;
Nay, more, an enemy unto you all,
And no great friend, I fear me, to the King.
Consider, lords, he is the next of blood
And heir apparent to the English crown.
Had Henry got an empire by his marriage
And all the wealthy kingdoms of the west,
There's reason he should be displeas'd at it.
Look to it, lords; let not his smoothing words
Bewitch your hearts; be wise and circumspect.
What though the common people favour him,
Calling him 'Humphrey, the good Duke of Gloucester,'
Clapping their hands, and crying with loud voice
'Jesu maintain your royal excellence!'
With 'God preserve the good Duke Humphrey!'
I fear me, lords, for all this flattering gloss,
He will be found a dangerous Protector.
BUCKINGHAM. Why should he then protect our sovereign,
He being of age to govern of himself?
Cousin of Somerset, join you with me,
And all together, with the Duke of Suffolk,
We'll quickly hoise Duke Humphrey from his seat.
CARDINAL. This weighty business will not brook delay;
I'll to the Duke of Suffolk presently. Exit
SOMERSET. Cousin of Buckingham, though Humphrey's pride
And greatness of his place be grief to us,
Yet let us watch the haughty cardinal;
His insolence is more intolerable
Than all the princes in the land beside;
If Gloucester be displac'd, he'll be Protector.

11

BUCKINGHAM. Or thou or I, Somerset, will be Protector,
  Despite Duke Humphrey or the Cardinal.
                    Exeunt BUCKINGHAM and SOMERSET
SALISBURY. Pride went before, ambition follows him.
  While these do labour for their own preferment,
  Behoves it us to labour for the realm.
  I never saw but Humphrey Duke of Gloucester
  Did bear him like a noble gentleman.
  Oft have I seen the haughty Cardinal-
  More like a soldier than a man o' th' church,
  As stout and proud as he were lord of all-
  Swear like a ruffian and demean himself
  Unlike the ruler of a commonweal.
  Warwick my son, the comfort of my age,
  Thy deeds, thy plainness, and thy housekeeping,
  Hath won the greatest favour of the commons,
  Excepting none but good Duke Humphrey.
  And, brother York, thy acts in Ireland,
  In bringing them to civil discipline,
  Thy late exploits done in the heart of France
  When thou wert Regent for our sovereign,
  Have made thee fear'd and honour'd of the people:
  Join we together for the public good,
  In what we can, to bridle and suppress
  The pride of Suffolk and the Cardinal,
  With Somerset's and Buckingham's ambition;
  And, as we may, cherish Duke Humphrey's deeds
  While they do tend the profit of the land.
WARWICK. So God help Warwick, as he loves the land
  And common profit of his country!
YORK. And so says York- [Aside] for he hath greatest cause.
SALISBURY. Then let's make haste away and look unto the main.
WARWICK. Unto the main! O father, Maine is lost-
  That Maine which by main force Warwick did win,
  And would have kept so long as breath did last.
  Main chance, father, you meant; but I meant Maine,
  Which I will win from France, or else be slain.
                    Exeunt WARWICK and SALISBURY
YORK. Anjou and Maine are given to the French;

12

Paris is lost; the state of Normandy
Stands on a tickle point now they are gone.
Suffolk concluded on the articles;
The peers agreed; and Henry was well pleas'd
To changes two dukedoms for a duke's fair daughter.
I cannot blame them all: what is't to them?
'Tis thine they give away, and not their own.
Pirates may make cheap pennyworths of their pillage,
And purchase friends, and give to courtezans,
Still revelling like lords till all be gone;
While as the silly owner of the goods
Weeps over them and wrings his hapless hands
And shakes his head and trembling stands aloof,
While all is shar'd and all is borne away,
Ready to starve and dare not touch his own.
So York must sit and fret and bite his tongue,
While his own lands are bargain'd for and sold.
Methinks the realms of England, France, and Ireland,
Bear that proportion to my flesh and blood
As did the fatal brand Althaea burnt
Unto the prince's heart of Calydon.
Anjou and Maine both given unto the French!
Cold news for me, for I had hope of France,
Even as I have of fertile England's soil.
A day will come when York shall claim his own;
And therefore I will take the Nevils' parts,
And make a show of love to proud Duke Humphrey,
And when I spy advantage, claim the crown,
For that's the golden mark I seek to hit.
Nor shall proud Lancaster usurp my right,
Nor hold the sceptre in his childish fist,
Nor wear the diadem upon his head,
Whose church-like humours fits not for a crown.
Then, York, be still awhile, till time do serve;
Watch thou and wake, when others be asleep,
To pry into the secrets of the state;
Till Henry, surfeiting in joys of love
With his new bride and England's dear-bought queen,
And Humphrey with the peers be fall'n at jars;

Then will I raise aloft the milk-white rose,
With whose sweet smell the air shall be perfum'd,
And in my standard bear the arms of York,
To grapple with the house of Lancaster;
And force perforce I'll make him yield the crown,
Whose bookish rule hath pull'd fair England down. Exit

SCENE II. The DUKE OF GLOUCESTER'S house

Enter DUKE and his wife ELEANOR

DUCHESS. Why droops my lord, like over-ripen'd corn
  Hanging the head at Ceres' plenteous load?
  Why doth the great Duke Humphrey knit his brows,
  As frowning at the favours of the world?
  Why are thine eyes fix'd to the sullen earth,
  Gazing on that which seems to dim thy sight?
  What see'st thou there? King Henry's diadem,
  Enchas'd with all the honours of the world?
  If so, gaze on, and grovel on thy face
  Until thy head be circled with the same.
  Put forth thy hand, reach at the glorious gold.
  What, is't too short? I'll lengthen it with mine;
  And having both together heav'd it up,
  We'll both together lift our heads to heaven,
  And never more abase our sight so low
  As to vouchsafe one glance unto the ground.
GLOUCESTER. O Nell, sweet Nell, if thou dost love thy lord,
  Banish the canker of ambitious thoughts!
  And may that thought, when I imagine ill
  Against my king and nephew, virtuous Henry,
  Be my last breathing in this mortal world!
  My troublous dreams this night doth make me sad.
DUCHESS. What dream'd my lord? Tell me, and I'll requite it
  With sweet rehearsal of my morning's dream.

GLOUCESTER. Methought this staff, mine office-badge in court,
  Was broke in twain; by whom I have forgot,
  But, as I think, it was by th' Cardinal;
  And on the pieces of the broken wand
  Were plac'd the heads of Edmund Duke of Somerset
  And William de la Pole, first Duke of Suffolk.
  This was my dream; what it doth bode God knows.
DUCHESS. Tut, this was nothing but an argument
  That he that breaks a stick of Gloucester's grove
  Shall lose his head for his presumption.
  But list to me, my Humphrey, my sweet Duke:
  Methought I sat in seat of majesty
  In the cathedral church of Westminster,
  And in that chair where kings and queens were crown'd;
  Where Henry and Dame Margaret kneel'd to me,
  And on my head did set the diadem.
GLOUCESTER. Nay, Eleanor, then must I chide outright.
  Presumptuous dame, ill-nurtur'd Eleanor!
  Art thou not second woman in the realm,
  And the Protector's wife, belov'd of him?
  Hast thou not worldly pleasure at command
  Above the reach or compass of thy thought?
  And wilt thou still be hammering treachery
  To tumble down thy husband and thyself
  From top of honour to disgrace's feet?
  Away from me, and let me hear no more!
DUCHESS. What, what, my lord! Are you so choleric
  With Eleanor for telling but her dream?
  Next time I'll keep my dreams unto myself
  And not be check'd.
GLOUCESTER. Nay, be not angry; I am pleas'd again.

Enter a MESSENGER

MESSENGER. My Lord Protector, 'tis his Highness' pleasure
  You do prepare to ride unto Saint Albans,
  Where as the King and Queen do mean to hawk.
GLOUCESTER. I go. Come, Nell, thou wilt ride with us?
DUCHESS. Yes, my good lord, I'll follow presently.

Follow I must; I cannot go before,
While Gloucester bears this base and humble mind.
Were I a man, a duke, and next of blood,
I would remove these tedious stumbling-blocks
And smooth my way upon their headless necks;
And, being a woman, I will not be slack
To play my part in Fortune's pageant.
Where are you there, Sir John? Nay, fear not, man,
We are alone; here's none but thee and I.

Enter HUME

HUME. Jesus preserve your royal Majesty!
DUCHESS. What say'st thou? Majesty! I am but Grace.
HUME. But, by the grace of God and Hume's advice,
  Your Grace's title shall be multiplied.
DUCHESS. What say'st thou, man? Hast thou as yet conferr'd
  With Margery Jourdain, the cunning witch of Eie,
  With Roger Bolingbroke, the conjurer?
  And will they undertake to do me good?
HUME. This they have promised, to show your Highness
  A spirit rais'd from depth of underground
  That shall make answer to such questions
  As by your Grace shall be propounded him
DUCHESS. It is enough; I'll think upon the questions;
  When from Saint Albans we do make return
  We'll see these things effected to the full.
  Here, Hume, take this reward; make merry, man,
  With thy confederates in this weighty cause. Exit
HUME. Hume must make merry with the Duchess' gold;
  Marry, and shall. But, how now, Sir John Hume!
  Seal up your lips and give no words but mum:
  The business asketh silent secrecy.
  Dame Eleanor gives gold to bring the witch:
  Gold cannot come amiss were she a devil.
  Yet have I gold flies from another coast-
  I dare not say from the rich Cardinal,
  And from the great and new-made Duke of Suffolk;

Yet I do find it so; for, to be plain,
They, knowing Dame Eleanor's aspiring humour,
Have hired me to undermine the Duchess,
And buzz these conjurations in her brain.
They say 'A crafty knave does need no broker';
Yet am I Suffolk and the Cardinal's broker.
Hume, if you take not heed, you shall go near
To call them both a pair of crafty knaves.
Well, so its stands; and thus, I fear, at last
Hume's knavery will be the Duchess' wreck,
And her attainture will be Humphrey's fall
Sort how it will, I shall have gold for all. Exit

SCENE III. London. The palace

Enter three or four PETITIONERS, PETER, the Armourer's man,
being one

  FIRST PETITIONER. My masters, let's stand close; my Lord
Protector
    will come this way by and by, and then we may deliver our
    supplications in the quill.
  SECOND PETITIONER. Marry, the Lord protect him, for he's a
good
    man, Jesu bless him!

Enter SUFFOLK and QUEEN

  FIRST PETITIONER. Here 'a comes, methinks, and the Queen
with him.
    I'll be the first, sure.
  SECOND PETITIONER. Come back, fool; this is the Duke of
Suffolk and
    not my Lord Protector.
  SUFFOLK. How now, fellow! Wouldst anything with me?
  FIRST PETITIONER. I pray, my lord, pardon me; I took ye for my

17

Lord
  Protector.
QUEEN. [Reads] 'To my Lord Protector!' Are your supplications to
  his lordship? Let me see them. What is thine?
FIRST PETITIONER. Mine is, an't please your Grace, against John
  Goodman, my Lord Cardinal's man, for keeping my house and
lands,
  and wife and all, from me.
SUFFOLK. Thy wife too! That's some wrong indeed. What's
yours?
  What's here! [Reads] 'Against the Duke of Suffolk, for enclosing
  the commons of Melford.' How now, sir knave!
SECOND PETITIONER. Alas, sir, I am but a poor petitioner of our
  whole township.
PETER. [Presenting his petition] Against my master, Thomas
Horner,
  for saying that the Duke of York was rightful heir to the crown.
QUEEN. What say'st thou? Did the Duke of York say he was
rightful
  heir to the crown?
PETER. That my master was? No, forsooth. My master said that he
  was, and that the King was an usurper.
SUFFOLK. Who is there? [Enter servant] Take this fellow in, and
  send for his master with a pursuivant presently. We'll hear more
  of your matter before the King.
                    Exit servant with PETER
QUEEN. And as for you, that love to be protected
  Under the wings of our Protector's grace,
  Begin your suits anew, and sue to him.
               [Tears the supplications]
  Away, base cullions! Suffolk, let them go.
ALL. Come, let's be gone. Exeunt
QUEEN. My Lord of Suffolk, say, is this the guise,
  Is this the fashions in the court of England?
  Is this the government of Britain's isle,
  And this the royalty of Albion's king?
  What, shall King Henry be a pupil still,
  Under the surly Gloucester's governance?
  Am I a queen in title and in style,

And must be made a subject to a duke?
I tell thee, Pole, when in the city Tours
Thou ran'st a tilt in honour of my love
And stol'st away the ladies' hearts of France,
I thought King Henry had resembled thee
In courage, courtship, and proportion;
But all his mind is bent to holiness,
To number Ave-Maries on his beads;
His champions are the prophets and apostles;
His weapons, holy saws of sacred writ;
His study is his tilt-yard, and his loves
Are brazen images of canonized saints.
I would the college of the Cardinals
Would choose him Pope, and carry him to Rome,
And set the triple crown upon his head;
That were a state fit for his holiness.
SUFFOLK. Madam, be patient. As I was cause
 Your Highness came to England, so will I
 In England work your Grace's full content.
QUEEN. Beside the haughty Protector, have we Beaufort
 The imperious churchman; Somerset, Buckingham,
 And grumbling York; and not the least of these
 But can do more in England than the King.
SUFFOLK. And he of these that can do most of all
 Cannot do more in England than the Nevils;
 Salisbury and Warwick are no simple peers.
QUEEN. Not all these lords do vex me half so much
 As that proud dame, the Lord Protector's wife.
 She sweeps it through the court with troops of ladies,
 More like an empress than Duke Humphrey's wife.
 Strangers in court do take her for the Queen.
 She bears a duke's revenues on her back,
 And in her heart she scorns our poverty;
 Shall I not live to be aveng'd on her?
 Contemptuous base-born callet as she is,
 She vaunted 'mongst her minions t' other day
 The very train of her worst wearing gown
 Was better worth than all my father's lands,
 Till Suffolk gave two dukedoms for his daughter.

SUFFOLK. Madam, myself have lim'd a bush for her,
  And plac'd a quire of such enticing birds
  That she will light to listen to the lays,
  And never mount to trouble you again.
  So, let her rest. And, madam, list to me,
  For I am bold to counsel you in this:
  Although we fancy not the Cardinal,
  Yet must we join with him and with the lords,
  Till we have brought Duke Humphrey in disgrace.
  As for the Duke of York, this late complaint
  Will make but little for his benefit.
  So one by one we'll weed them all at last,
  And you yourself shall steer the happy helm.

       Sound a sennet. Enter the KING, DUKE HUMPHREY,
    CARDINAL BEAUFORT, BUCKINGHAM, YORK,
  SOMERSET, SALISBURY,
          WARWICK, and the DUCHESS OF GLOUCESTER

KING HENRY. For my part, noble lords, I care not which:
  Or Somerset or York, all's one to me.
YORK. If York have ill demean'd himself in France,
  Then let him be denay'd the regentship.
SOMERSET. If Somerset be unworthy of the place,
  Let York be Regent; I will yield to him.
WARWICK. Whether your Grace be worthy, yea or no,
  Dispute not that; York is the worthier.
CARDINAL. Ambitious Warwick, let thy betters speak.
WARWICK. The Cardinal's not my better in the field.
BUCKINGHAM. All in this presence are thy betters, Warwick.
WARWICK. Warwick may live to be the best of all.
SALISBURY. Peace, son! And show some reason, Buckingham,
  Why Somerset should be preferr'd in this.
QUEEN. Because the King, forsooth, will have it so.
GLOUCESTER. Madam, the King is old enough himself
  To give his censure. These are no women's matters.
QUEEN. If he be old enough, what needs your Grace
  To be Protector of his Excellence?
GLOUCESTER. Madam, I am Protector of the realm;

And at his pleasure will resign my place.
SUFFOLK. Resign it then, and leave thine insolence.
  Since thou wert king- as who is king but thou?-
  The commonwealth hath daily run to wrack,
  The Dauphin hath prevail'd beyond the seas,
  And all the peers and nobles of the realm
  Have been as bondmen to thy sovereignty.
CARDINAL. The commons hast thou rack'd; the clergy's bags
  Are lank and lean with thy extortions.
SOMERSET. Thy sumptuous buildings and thy wife's attire
  Have cost a mass of public treasury.
BUCKINGHAM. Thy cruelty in execution
  Upon offenders hath exceeded law,
  And left thee to the mercy of the law.
QUEEN. Thy sale of offices and towns in France,
  If they were known, as the suspect is great,
  Would make thee quickly hop without thy head.
            Exit GLOUCESTER. The QUEEN drops QUEEN her
fan
  Give me my fan. What, minion, can ye not?
            [She gives the DUCHESS a box on the ear]
  I cry your mercy, madam; was it you?
DUCHESS. Was't I? Yea, I it was, proud Frenchwoman.
  Could I come near your beauty with my nails,
  I could set my ten commandments in your face.
KING HENRY. Sweet aunt, be quiet; 'twas against her will.
DUCHESS. Against her will, good King? Look to 't in time;
  She'll hamper thee and dandle thee like a baby.
  Though in this place most master wear no breeches,
  She shall not strike Dame Eleanor unreveng'd. Exit
BUCKINGHAM. Lord Cardinal, I will follow Eleanor,
  And listen after Humphrey, how he proceeds.
  She's tickled now; her fume needs no spurs,
  She'll gallop far enough to her destruction. Exit

Re-enter GLOUCESTER

GLOUCESTER. Now, lords, my choler being overblown
  With walking once about the quadrangle,

21

I come to talk of commonwealth affairs.
As for your spiteful false objections,
Prove them, and I lie open to the law;
But God in mercy so deal with my soul
As I in duty love my king and country!
But to the matter that we have in hand:
I say, my sovereign, York is meetest man
To be your Regent in the realm of France.
SUFFOLK. Before we make election, give me leave
  To show some reason, of no little force,
  That York is most unmeet of any man.
YORK. I'll tell thee, Suffolk, why I am unmeet:
  First, for I cannot flatter thee in pride;
  Next, if I be appointed for the place,
  My Lord of Somerset will keep me here
  Without discharge, money, or furniture,
  Till France be won into the Dauphin's hands.
  Last time I danc'd attendance on his will
  Till Paris was besieg'd, famish'd, and lost.
WARWICK. That can I witness; and a fouler fact
  Did never traitor in the land commit.
SUFFOLK. Peace, headstrong Warwick!
WARWICK. Image of pride, why should I hold my peace?

Enter HORNER, the Armourer, and his man PETER, guarded

SUFFOLK. Because here is a man accus'd of treason:
  Pray God the Duke of York excuse himself!
YORK. Doth any one accuse York for a traitor?
KING HENRY. What mean'st thou, Suffolk? Tell me, what are
these?
SUFFOLK. Please it your Majesty, this is the man
  That doth accuse his master of high treason;
  His words were these: that Richard Duke of York
  Was rightful heir unto the English crown,
  And that your Majesty was an usurper.
KING HENRY. Say, man, were these thy words?
HORNER. An't shall please your Majesty, I never said nor thought
  any such matter. God is my witness, I am falsely accus'd by the

villain.

PETER. [Holding up his hands] By these ten bones, my lords, he did

    speak them to me in the garret one night, as we were scouring my
    Lord of York's armour.

YORK. Base dunghill villain and mechanical,
    I'll have thy head for this thy traitor's speech.
    I do beseech your royal Majesty,
    Let him have all the rigour of the law.

HORNER`. Alas, my lord, hang me if ever I spake the words. My
    accuser is my prentice; and when I did correct him for his fault
    the other day, he did vow upon his knees he would be even with
    me. I have good witness of this; therefore I beseech your
    Majesty, do not cast away an honest man for a villain's
    accusation.

KING HENRY. Uncle, what shall we say to this in law?

GLOUCESTER. This doom, my lord, if I may judge:
    Let Somerset be Regent o'er the French,
    Because in York this breeds suspicion;
    And let these have a day appointed them
    For single combat in convenient place,
    For he hath witness of his servant's malice.
    This is the law, and this Duke Humphrey's doom.

SOMERSET. I humbly thank your royal Majesty.

HORNER. And I accept the combat willingly.

PETER. Alas, my lord, I cannot fight; for God's sake, pity my case!
    The spite of man prevaileth against me. O Lord, have mercy upon
    me, I shall never be able to fight a blow! O Lord, my heart!

GLOUCESTER. Sirrah, or you must fight or else be hang'd.

KING HENRY. Away with them to prison; and the day of combat shall

    be the last of the next month.
    Come, Somerset, we'll see thee sent away. Flourish. Exeunt

SCENE IV. London. The DUKE OF GLOUCESTER'S

garden

Enter MARGERY JOURDAIN, the witch; the two priests, HUME and SOUTHWELL; and BOLINGBROKE

HUME. Come, my masters; the Duchess, I tell you, expects
  performance of your promises.
BOLINGBROKE. Master Hume, we are therefore provided; will her
  ladyship behold and hear our exorcisms?
HUME. Ay, what else? Fear you not her courage.
BOLINGBROKE. I have heard her reported to be a woman of an
  invincible spirit; but it shall be convenient, Master Hume, that
  you be by her aloft while we be busy below; and so I pray you go,
  in God's name, and leave us. [Exit HUME] Mother Jourdain, be you
  prostrate and grovel on the earth; John Southwell, read you; and
  let us to our work.

Enter DUCHESS aloft, followed by HUME

DUCHESS. Well said, my masters; and welcome all. To this gear, the
  sooner the better.
BOLINGBROKE. Patience, good lady; wizards know their times:
  Deep night, dark night, the silent of the night,
  The time of night when Troy was set on fire;
  The time when screech-owls cry and ban-dogs howl,
  And spirits walk and ghosts break up their graves-
  That time best fits the work we have in hand.
  Madam, sit you, and fear not: whom we raise
  We will make fast within a hallow'd verge.

  [Here they do the ceremonies belonging, and make the circle;
      BOLINGBROKE or SOUTHWELL reads: 'Conjuro te,' &c.
  It thunders and lightens terribly; then the SPIRIT riseth]

SPIRIT. Adsum.
MARGERY JOURDAIN. Asmath,

24

By the eternal God, whose name and power
Thou tremblest at, answer that I shall ask;
For till thou speak thou shalt not pass from hence.
SPIRIT. Ask what thou wilt; that I had said and done.
BOLINGBROKE. [Reads] 'First of the king: what shall of him become?'
SPIRIT. The Duke yet lives that Henry shall depose;
But him outlive, and die a violent death.

   [As the SPIRIT speaks, SOUTHWELL writes the answer]
BOLINGBROKE. 'What fates await the Duke of Suffolk?'
SPIRIT. By water shall he die and take his end.
BOLINGBROKE. 'What shall befall the Duke of Somerset?'
SPIRIT. Let him shun castles:
Safer shall he be upon the sandy plains
Than where castles mounted stand.
Have done, for more I hardly can endure.
BOLINGBROKE. Descend to darkness and the burning lake;
False fiend, avoid! Thunder and lightning. Exit SPIRIT

   Enter the DUKE OF YORK and the DUKE OF
    BUCKINGHAM with guard, and break in

YORK. Lay hands upon these traitors and their trash.
Beldam, I think we watch'd you at an inch.
What, madam, are you there? The King and commonweal
Are deeply indebted for this piece of pains;
My Lord Protector will, I doubt it not,
See you well guerdon'd for these good deserts.
DUCHESS. Not half so bad as thine to England's king,
Injurious Duke, that threatest where's no cause.
BUCKINGHAM. True, madam, none at all. What can you this?
Away with them! let them be clapp'd up close,
And kept asunder. You, madam, shall with us.
Stafford, take her to thee.
We'll see your trinkets here all forthcoming.
All, away!

   Exeunt, above, DUCHESS and HUME, guarded; below,
    WITCH, SOUTHWELL and BOLINGBROKE,
guarded

YORK. Lord Buckingham, methinks you watch'd her well.
  A pretty plot, well chosen to build upon!
  Now, pray, my lord, let's see the devil's writ.
  What have we here? [Reads]
  'The duke yet lives that Henry shall depose;
  But him outlive, and die a violent death.'
  Why, this is just
  'Aio te, Aeacida, Romanos vincere posse.'
  Well, to the rest:
  'Tell me what fate awaits the Duke of Suffolk?'
  'By water shall he die and take his end.'
  'What shall betide the Duke of Somerset?'
  'Let him shun castles;
  Safer shall he be upon the sandy plains
  Than where castles mounted stand.'
  Come, come, my lords;
  These oracles are hardly attain'd,
  And hardly understood.
  The King is now in progress towards Saint Albans,
  With him the husband of this lovely lady;
  Thither go these news as fast as horse can carry them-
  A sorry breakfast for my Lord Protector.
  BUCKINGHAM. Your Grace shall give me leave, my Lord of York,
  To be the post, in hope of his reward.
  YORK. At your pleasure, my good lord.
  Who's within there, ho?

Enter a serving-man

  Invite my Lords of Salisbury and Warwick
  To sup with me to-morrow night. Away! Exeunt

ACT II. SCENE I. Saint Albans

Enter the KING, QUEEN, GLOUCESTER, CARDINAL, and
SUFFOLK, with Falconers halloing

26

QUEEN. Believe me, lords, for flying at the brook,
  I saw not better sport these seven years' day;
  Yet, by your leave, the wind was very high,
  And ten to one old Joan had not gone out.
KING HENRY. But what a point, my lord, your falcon made,
  And what a pitch she flew above the rest!
  To see how God in all His creatures works!
  Yea, man and birds are fain of climbing high.
SUFFOLK. No marvel, an it like your Majesty,
  My Lord Protector's hawks do tow'r so well;
  They know their master loves to be aloft,
  And bears his thoughts above his falcon's pitch.
GLOUCESTER. My lord, 'tis but a base ignoble mind
  That mounts no higher than a bird can soar.
CARDINAL. I thought as much; he would be above the clouds.
GLOUCESTER. Ay, my lord Cardinal, how think you by that?
  Were it not good your Grace could fly to heaven?
KING HENRY. The treasury of everlasting joy!
CARDINAL. Thy heaven is on earth; thine eyes and thoughts
  Beat on a crown, the treasure of thy heart;
  Pernicious Protector, dangerous peer,
  That smooth'st it so with King and commonweal.
GLOUCESTER. What, Cardinal, is your priesthood grown
peremptory?
  Tantaene animis coelestibus irae?
  Churchmen so hot? Good uncle, hide such malice;
  With such holiness can you do it?
SUFFOLK. No malice, sir; no more than well becomes
  So good a quarrel and so bad a peer.
GLOUCESTER. As who, my lord?
SUFFOLK. Why, as you, my lord,
  An't like your lordly Lord's Protectorship.
GLOUCESTER. Why, Suffolk, England knows thine insolence.
QUEEN. And thy ambition, Gloucester.
KING HENRY. I prithee, peace,
  Good Queen, and whet not on these furious peers;
  For blessed are the peacemakers on earth.
CARDINAL. Let me be blessed for the peace I make
  Against this proud Protector with my sword!

GLOUCESTER. [Aside to CARDINAL] Faith, holy uncle, would 'twere
  come to that!
CARDINAL. [Aside to GLOUCESTER] Marry, when thou dar'st.
GLOUCESTER. [Aside to CARDINAL] Make up no factious numbers for the
   matter;
  In thine own person answer thy abuse.
CARDINAL. [Aside to GLOUCESTER] Ay, where thou dar'st not peep; an
   if thou dar'st,
  This evening on the east side of the grove.
KING HENRY. How now, my lords!
CARDINAL. Believe me, cousin Gloucester,
  Had not your man put up the fowl so suddenly,
  We had had more sport. [Aside to GLOUCESTER] Come with thy
   two-hand sword.
GLOUCESTER. True, uncle.
CARDINAL. [Aside to GLOUCESTER] Are ye advis'd? The east side of
  the grove?
GLOUCESTER. [Aside to CARDINAL] Cardinal, I am with you.
KING HENRY. Why, how now, uncle Gloucester!
GLOUCESTER. Talking of hawking; nothing else, my lord.
  [Aside to CARDINAL] Now, by God's Mother, priest,
  I'll shave your crown for this,
  Or all my fence shall fail.
CARDINAL. [Aside to GLOUCESTER] Medice, teipsum;
  Protector, see to't well; protect yourself.
KING HENRY. The winds grow high; so do your stomachs, lords.
  How irksome is this music to my heart!
  When such strings jar, what hope of harmony?
  I pray, my lords, let me compound this strife.

Enter a TOWNSMAN of Saint Albans, crying 'A miracle!'

GLOUCESTER. What means this noise?
  Fellow, what miracle dost thou proclaim?

28

TOWNSMAN. A miracle! A miracle!

SUFFOLK. Come to the King, and tell him what miracle.

TOWNSMAN. Forsooth, a blind man at Saint Albans shrine
  Within this half hour hath receiv'd his sight;
  A man that ne'er saw in his life before.

KING HENRY. Now God be prais'd that to believing souls
  Gives light in darkness, comfort in despair!

  Enter the MAYOR OF SAINT ALBANS and his brethren,
    bearing Simpcox between two in a chair;
    his WIFE and a multitude following

CARDINAL. Here comes the townsmen on procession
  To present your Highness with the man.

KING HENRY. Great is his comfort in this earthly vale,
  Although by his sight his sin be multiplied.

GLOUCESTER. Stand by, my masters; bring him near the King;
  His Highness' pleasure is to talk with him.

KING HENRY. Good fellow, tell us here the circumstance,
  That we for thee may glorify the Lord.
  What, hast thou been long blind and now restor'd?

SIMPCOX. Born blind, an't please your Grace.

WIFE. Ay indeed was he.

SUFFOLK. What woman is this?

WIFE. His wife, an't like your worship.

GLOUCESTER. Hadst thou been his mother, thou couldst have better
  told.

KING HENRY. Where wert thou born?

SIMPCOX. At Berwick in the north, an't like your Grace.

KING HENRY. Poor soul, God's goodness hath been great to thee.
  Let never day nor night unhallowed pass,
  But still remember what the Lord hath done.

QUEEN. Tell me, good fellow, cam'st thou here by chance,
  Or of devotion, to this holy shrine?

SIMPCOX. God knows, of pure devotion; being call'd
  A hundred times and oft'ner, in my sleep,
  By good Saint Alban, who said 'Simpcox, come,
  Come, offer at my shrine, and I will help thee.'

29

WIFE. Most true, forsooth; and many time and oft
  Myself have heard a voice to call him so.
CARDINAL. What, art thou lame?
SIMPCOX. Ay, God Almighty help me!
SUFFOLK. How cam'st thou so?
SIMPCOX. A fall off of a tree.
WIFE. A plum tree, master.
GLOUCESTER. How long hast thou been blind?
SIMPCOX. O, born so, master!
GLOUCESTER. What, and wouldst climb a tree?
SIMPCOX. But that in all my life, when I was a youth.
WIFE. Too true; and bought his climbing very dear.
GLOUCESTER. Mass, thou lov'dst plums well, that wouldst
venture so.
SIMPCOX. Alas, good master, my wife desir'd some damsons
  And made me climb, With danger of my life.
GLOUCESTER. A subtle knave! But yet it shall not serve:
  Let me see thine eyes; wink now; now open them;
  In my opinion yet thou seest not well.
SIMPCOX. Yes, master, clear as day, I thank God and Saint Alban.
GLOUCESTER. Say'st thou me so? What colour is this cloak of?
SIMPCOX. Red, master; red as blood.
GLOUCESTER. Why, that's well said. What colour is my gown
of?
SIMPCOX. Black, forsooth; coal-black as jet.
KING HENRY. Why, then, thou know'st what colour jet is of?
SUFFOLK. And yet, I think, jet did he never see.
GLOUCESTER. But cloaks and gowns before this day a many.
WIFE. Never before this day in all his life.
GLOUCESTER. Tell me, sirrah, what's my name?
SIMPCOX. Alas, master, I know not.
GLOUCESTER. What's his name?
SIMPCOX. I know not.
GLOUCESTER. Nor his?
SIMPCOX. No, indeed, master.
GLOUCESTER. What's thine own name?
SIMPCOX. Saunder Simpcox, an if it please you, master.
GLOUCESTER. Then, Saunder, sit there, the lying'st knave in
  Christendom. If thou hadst been born blind, thou mightst as well

have known all our names as thus to name the several colours we do wear. Sight may distinguish of colours; but suddenly to nominate them all, it is impossible. My lords, Saint Alban here hath done a miracle; and would ye not think his cunning to be great that could restore this cripple to his legs again?

SIMPCOX. O master, that you could!

GLOUCESTER. My masters of Saint Albans, have you not beadles in
  your town, and things call'd whips?

MAYOR. Yes, my lord, if it please your Grace.

GLOUCESTER. Then send for one presently.

MAYOR. Sirrah, go fetch the beadle hither straight.
                    Exit an attendant

GLOUCESTER. Now fetch me a stool hither by and by. [A stool
  brought] Now, sirrah, if you mean to save yourself from whipping,
  leap me over this stool and run away.

SIMPCOX. Alas, master, I am not able to stand alone!
  You go about to torture me in vain.

Enter a BEADLE with whips

GLOUCESTER. Well, sir, we must have you find your legs.
  Sirrah beadle, whip him till he leap over that same stool.

BEADLE. I will, my lord. Come on, sirrah; off with your doublet
  quickly.

SIMPCOX. Alas, master, what shall I do? I am not able to stand.

> *After the BEADLE hath hit him once, he leaps over*
> *the stool and runs away; and they follow and cry*
> *'A miracle!'*

KING HENRY. O God, seest Thou this, and bearest so long?

QUEEN. It made me laugh to see the villain run.

GLOUCESTER. Follow the knave, and take this drab away.

WIFE. Alas, sir, we did it for pure need!

GLOUCESTER. Let them be whipp'd through every market town till they
  come to Berwick, from whence they came.
                    Exeunt MAYOR, BEADLE, WIFE, &c.

31

CARDINAL. Duke Humphrey has done a miracle to-day.
SUFFOLK. True; made the lame to leap and fly away.
GLOUCESTER. But you have done more miracles than I:
  You made in a day, my lord, whole towns to fly.

Enter BUCKINGHAM

KING HENRY. What tidings with our cousin Buckingham?
BUCKINGHAM. Such as my heart doth tremble to unfold:
  A sort of naughty persons, lewdly bent,
  Under the countenance and confederacy
  Of Lady Eleanor, the Protector's wife,
  The ringleader and head of all this rout,
  Have practis'd dangerously against your state,
  Dealing with witches and with conjurers,
  Whom we have apprehended in the fact,
  Raising up wicked spirits from under ground,
  Demanding of King Henry's life and death
  And other of your Highness' Privy Council,
  As more at large your Grace shall understand.
CARDINAL. And so, my Lord Protector, by this means
  Your lady is forthcoming yet at London.
  This news, I think, hath turn'd your weapon's edge;
  'Tis like, my lord, you will not keep your hour.
GLOUCESTER. Ambitious churchman, leave to afflict my heart.
  Sorrow and grief have vanquish'd all my powers;
  And, vanquish'd as I am, I yield to the
  Or to the meanest groom.
KING HENRY. O God, what mischiefs work the wicked ones,
  Heaping confusion on their own heads thereby!
QUEEN. Gloucester, see here the tainture of thy nest;
  And look thyself be faultless, thou wert best.
GLOUCESTER. Madam, for myself, to heaven I do appeal
  How I have lov'd my King and commonweal;
  And for my wife I know not how it stands.
  Sorry I am to hear what I have heard.
  Noble she is; but if she have forgot
  Honour and virtue, and convers'd with such
  As, like to pitch, defile nobility,

I banish her my bed and company
And give her as a prey to law and shame,
That hath dishonoured Gloucester's honest name.
KING HENRY. Well, for this night we will repose us here.
To-morrow toward London back again
To look into this business thoroughly
And call these foul offenders to their answers,
And poise the cause in justice' equal scales,
Whose beam stands sure, whose rightful cause prevails.
                              Flourish. Exeunt

SCENE II. London. The DUKE OF YORK'S garden

Enter YORK, SALISBURY, and WARWICK

YORK. Now, my good Lords of Salisbury and Warwick,
  Our simple supper ended, give me leave
  In this close walk to satisfy myself
  In craving your opinion of my tide,
  Which is infallible, to England's crown.
SALISBURY. My lord, I long to hear it at full.
WARWICK. Sweet York, begin; and if thy claim be good,
  The Nevils are thy subjects to command.
YORK. Then thus:
  Edward the Third, my lords, had seven sons;
  The first, Edward the Black Prince, Prince of Wales;
  The second, William of Hatfield; and the third,
  Lionel Duke of Clarence; next to whom
  Was John of Gaunt, the Duke of Lancaster;
  The fifth was Edmund Langley, Duke of York;
  The sixth was Thomas of Woodstock, Duke of Gloucester;
  William of Windsor was the seventh and last.
  Edward the Black Prince died before his father
  And left behind him Richard, his only son,
  Who, after Edward the Third's death, reign'd as king

Till Henry Bolingbroke, Duke of Lancaster,
The eldest son and heir of John of Gaunt,
Crown'd by the name of Henry the Fourth,
Seiz'd on the realm, depos'd the rightful king,
Sent his poor queen to France, from whence she came.
And him to Pomfret, where, as all you know,
Harmless Richard was murdered traitorously.
WARWICK. Father, the Duke hath told the truth;
Thus got the house of Lancaster the crown.
YORK. Which now they hold by force, and not by right;
For Richard, the first son's heir, being dead,
The issue of the next son should have reign'd.
SALISBURY. But William of Hatfield died without an heir.
YORK. The third son, Duke of Clarence, from whose line
I claim the crown, had issue Philippe, a daughter,
Who married Edmund Mortimer, Earl of March;
Edmund had issue, Roger Earl of March;
Roger had issue, Edmund, Anne, and Eleanor.
SALISBURY. This Edmund, in the reign of Bolingbroke,
As I have read, laid claim unto the crown;
And, but for Owen Glendower, had been king,
Who kept him in captivity till he died.
But, to the rest.
YORK. His eldest sister, Anne,
My mother, being heir unto the crown,
Married Richard Earl of Cambridge, who was
To Edmund Langley, Edward the Third's fifth son, son.
By her I claim the kingdom: she was heir
To Roger Earl of March, who was the son
Of Edmund Mortimer, who married Philippe,
Sole daughter unto Lionel Duke of Clarence;
So, if the issue of the elder son
Succeed before the younger, I am King.
WARWICK. What plain proceedings is more plain than this?
Henry doth claim the crown from John of Gaunt,
The fourth son: York claims it from the third.
Till Lionel's issue fails, his should not reign.
It fails not yet, but flourishes in thee
And in thy sons, fair slips of such a stock.

Then, father Salisbury, kneel we together,
And in this private plot be we the first
That shall salute our rightful sovereign
With honour of his birthright to the crown.
BOTH. Long live our sovereign Richard, England's King!
YORK. We thank you, lords. But I am not your king
  Till I be crown'd, and that my sword be stain'd
  With heart-blood of the house of Lancaster;
  And that's not suddenly to be perform'd,
  But with advice and silent secrecy.
  Do you as I do in these dangerous days:
  Wink at the Duke of Suffolk's insolence,
  At Beaufort's pride, at Somerset's ambition,
  At Buckingham, and all the crew of them,
  Till they have snar'd the shepherd of the flock,
  That virtuous prince, the good Duke Humphrey;
  'Tis that they seek; and they, in seeking that,
  Shall find their deaths, if York can prophesy.
SALISBURY. My lord, break we off; we know your mind at full.
WARWICK. My heart assures me that the Earl of Warwick
  Shall one day make the Duke of York a king.
YORK. And, Nevil, this I do assure myself,
  Richard shall live to make the Earl of Warwick
  The greatest man in England but the King. Exeunt

SCENE III. London. A hall of justice

Sound trumpets. Enter the KING and State: the QUEEN,
GLOUCESTER, YORK, SUFFOLK, and SALISBURY, with guard,
to banish the DUCHESS. Enter, guarded, the DUCHESS OF
GLOUCESTER, MARGERY JOURDAIN, HUME, SOUTHWELL,
and BOLINGBROKE

  KING HENRY. Stand forth, Dame Eleanor Cobham, Gloucester's
wife:

In sight of God and us, your guilt is great;
Receive the sentence of the law for sins
Such as by God's book are adjudg'd to death.
You four, from hence to prison back again;
From thence unto the place of execution:
The witch in Smithfield shall be burnt to ashes,
And you three shall be strangled on the gallows.
You, madam, for you are more nobly born,
Despoiled of your honour in your life,
Shall, after three days' open penance done,
Live in your country here in banishment
With Sir John Stanley in the Isle of Man.
DUCHESS. Welcome is banishment; welcome were my death.
GLOUCESTER. Eleanor, the law, thou seest, hath judged thee.
  I cannot justify whom the law condemns.
       Exeunt the DUCHESS and the other prisoners, guarded
  Mine eyes are full of tears, my heart of grief.
  Ah, Humphrey, this dishonour in thine age
  Will bring thy head with sorrow to the ground!
  I beseech your Majesty give me leave to go;
  Sorrow would solace, and mine age would ease.
KING HENRY. Stay, Humphrey Duke of Gloucester; ere thou go,
  Give up thy staff; Henry will to himself
  Protector be; and God shall be my hope,
  My stay, my guide, and lantern to my feet.
  And go in peace, Humphrey, no less belov'd
  Than when thou wert Protector to thy King.
QUEEN. I see no reason why a king of years
  Should be to be protected like a child.
  God and King Henry govern England's realm!
  Give up your staff, sir, and the King his realm.
GLOUCESTER. My staff! Here, noble Henry, is my staff.
  As willingly do I the same resign
  As ere thy father Henry made it mine;
  And even as willingly at thy feet I leave it
  As others would ambitiously receive it.
  Farewell, good King; when I am dead and gone,
  May honourable peace attend thy throne! Exit
QUEEN. Why, now is Henry King, and Margaret Queen,

And Humphrey Duke of Gloucester scarce himself,
That bears so shrewd a maim: two pulls at once-
His lady banish'd and a limb lopp'd off.
This staff of honour raught, there let it stand
Where it best fits to be, in Henry's hand.
SUFFOLK. Thus droops this lofty pine and hangs his sprays;
Thus Eleanor's pride dies in her youngest days.
YORK. Lords, let him go. Please it your Majesty,
This is the day appointed for the combat;
And ready are the appellant and defendant,
The armourer and his man, to enter the lists,
So please your Highness to behold the fight.
QUEEN. Ay, good my lord; for purposely therefore
Left I the court, to see this quarrel tried.
KING HENRY. A God's name, see the lists and all things fit;
Here let them end it, and God defend the right!
YORK. I never saw a fellow worse bested,
Or more afraid to fight, than is the appellant,
The servant of his armourer, my lords.

    Enter at one door, HORNER, the Armourer, and his
     NEIGHBOURS, drinking to him so much that he is
     drunk; and he enters with a drum before him and
     his staff with a sand-bag fastened to it; and at the
     other door PETER, his man, with a drum and sandbag,
        and PRENTICES drinking to him

FIRST NEIGHBOUR. Here, neighbour Horner, I drink to you in a cup of
  sack; and fear not, neighbour, you shall do well enough.
SECOND NEIGHBOUR. And here, neighbour, here's a cup of charneco.
THIRD NEIGHBOUR. And here's a pot of good double beer, neighbour;
  drink, and fear not your man.
HORNER. Let it come, i' faith, and I'll pledge you all; and a fig
  for Peter!
FIRST PRENTICE. Here, Peter, I drink to thee; and be not afraid.
SECOND PRENTICE. Be merry, Peter, and fear not thy master:

fight
for credit of the prentices.

PETER. I thank you all. Drink, and pray for me, I pray you; for I
think I have taken my last draught in this world. Here, Robin, an
if I die, I give thee my apron; and, Will, thou shalt have my
hammer; and here, Tom, take all the money that I have. O Lord
bless me, I pray God! for I am never able to deal with my master,
he hath learnt so much fence already.

SALISBURY. Come, leave your drinking and fall to blows.
Sirrah, what's thy name?

PETER. Peter, forsooth.

SALISBURY. Peter? What more?

PETER. Thump.

SALISBURY. Thump? Then see thou thump thy master well.

HORNER. Masters, I am come hither, as it were, upon my man's
instigation, to prove him a knave and myself an honest man; and
touching the Duke of York, I will take my death I never meant
him
any ill, nor the King, nor the Queen; and therefore, Peter, have
at thee with a down right blow!

YORK. Dispatch- this knave's tongue begins to double.
Sound, trumpets, alarum to the combatants!

[Alarum. They fight and PETER strikes him down]

HORNER. Hold, Peter, hold! I confess, I confess treason.

[Dies]

YORK. Take away his weapon. Fellow, thank God, and the good
wine in
thy master's way.

PETER. O God, have I overcome mine enemies in this presence? O
Peter, thou hast prevail'd in right!

KING HENRY. Go, take hence that traitor from our sight,
For by his death we do perceive his guilt;
And God in justice hath reveal'd to us
The truth and innocence of this poor fellow,
Which he had thought to have murder'd wrongfully.
Come, fellow, follow us for thy reward.

Sound a flourish. Exeunt

38

SCENE IV. *London. A street*

Enter DUKE HUMPHREY and his men, in mourning cloaks

GLOUCESTER. Thus sometimes hath the brightest day a cloud,
 And after summer evermore succeeds
 Barren winter, with his wrathful nipping cold;
 So cares and joys abound, as seasons fleet.
 Sirs, what's o'clock?
SERVING-MAN. Ten, my lord.
GLOUCESTER. Ten is the hour that was appointed me
 To watch the coming of my punish'd duchess.
 Uneath may she endure the flinty streets
 To tread them with her tender-feeling feet.
 Sweet Nell, ill can thy noble mind abrook
 The abject people gazing on thy face,
 With envious looks, laughing at thy shame,
 That erst did follow thy proud chariot wheels
 When thou didst ride in triumph through the streets.
 But, soft! I think she comes, and I'll prepare
 My tear-stain'd eyes to see her miseries.

> Enter the DUCHESS OF GLOUCESTER in a white sheet,
> and a taper burning in her hand, with SIR JOHN
> STANLEY, the SHERIFF, and OFFICERS

SERVING-MAN. So please your Grace, we'll take her from the
sheriff.
GLOUCESTER. No, stir not for your lives; let her pass by.
DUCHESS. Come you, my lord, to see my open shame?
 Now thou dost penance too. Look how they gaze!
 See how the giddy multitude do point
 And nod their heads and throw their eyes on thee;
 Ah, Gloucester, hide thee from their hateful looks,
 And, in thy closet pent up, rue my shame
 And ban thine enemies, both mine and thine!
GLOUCESTER. Be patient, gentle Nell; forget this grief.
DUCHESS. Ah, Gloucester, teach me to forget myself!
 For whilst I think I am thy married wife

And thou a prince, Protector of this land,
Methinks I should not thus be led along,
Mail'd up in shame, with papers on my back,
And follow'd with a rabble that rejoice
To see my tears and hear my deep-fet groans.
The ruthless flint doth cut my tender feet,
And when I start, the envious people laugh
And bid me be advised how I tread.
Ah, Humphrey, can I bear this shameful yoke?
Trowest thou that e'er I'll look upon the world
Or count them happy that enjoy the sun?
No; dark shall be my light and night my day;
To think upon my pomp shall be my hell.
Sometimes I'll say I am Duke Humphrey's wife,
And he a prince, and ruler of the land;
Yet so he rul'd, and such a prince he was,
As he stood by whilst I, his forlorn duchess,
Was made a wonder and a pointing-stock
To every idle rascal follower.
But be thou mild, and blush not at my shame,
Nor stir at nothing till the axe of death
Hang over thee, as sure it shortly will.
For Suffolk- he that can do all in all
With her that hateth thee and hates us all-
And York, and impious Beaufort, that false priest,
Have all lim'd bushes to betray thy wings,
And, fly thou how thou canst, they'll tangle thee.
But fear not thou until thy foot be snar'd,
Nor never seek prevention of thy foes.
GLOUCESTER. Ah, Nell, forbear! Thou aimest all awry.
I must offend before I be attainted;
And had I twenty times so many foes,
And each of them had twenty times their power,
All these could not procure me any scathe
So long as I am loyal, true, and crimeless.
Wouldst have me rescue thee from this reproach?
Why, yet thy scandal were not wip'd away,
But I in danger for the breach of law.
Thy greatest help is quiet, gentle Nell.

I pray thee sort thy heart to patience;
These few days' wonder will be quickly worn.

Enter a HERALD

HERALD. I summon your Grace to his Majesty's Parliament,
  Holden at Bury the first of this next month.
GLOUCESTER. And my consent ne'er ask'd herein before!
  This is close dealing. Well, I will be there. Exit HERALD
  My Nell, I take my leave- and, master sheriff,
  Let not her penance exceed the King's commission.
SHERIFF. An't please your Grace, here my commission stays;
  And Sir John Stanley is appointed now
  To take her with him to the Isle of Man.
GLOUCESTER. Must you, Sir John, protect my lady here?
STANLEY. So am I given in charge, may't please your Grace.
GLOUCESTER. Entreat her not the worse in that I pray
  You use her well; the world may laugh again,
  And I may live to do you kindness if
  You do it her. And so, Sir John, farewell.
DUCHESS. What, gone, my lord, and bid me not farewell!
GLOUCESTER. Witness my tears, I cannot stay to speak.
                    Exeunt GLOUCESTER and servants
DUCHESS. Art thou gone too? All comfort go with thee!
  For none abides with me. My joy is death-
  Death, at whose name I oft have been afeard,
  Because I wish'd this world's eternity.
  Stanley, I prithee go, and take me hence;
  I care not whither, for I beg no favour,
  Only convey me where thou art commanded.
STANLEY. Why, madam, that is to the Isle of Man,
  There to be us'd according to your state.
DUCHESS. That's bad enough, for I am but reproach-
  And shall I then be us'd reproachfully?
STANLEY. Like to a duchess and Duke Humphrey's lady;
  According to that state you shall be us'd.
DUCHESS. Sheriff, farewell, and better than I fare,
  Although thou hast been conduct of my shame.
SHERIFF. It is my office; and, madam, pardon me.

41

DUCHESS. Ay, ay, farewell; thy office is discharg'd.
  Come, Stanley, shall we go?
STANLEY. Madam, your penance done, throw off this sheet,
  And go we to attire you for our journey.
DUCHESS. My shame will not be shifted with my sheet.
  No, it will hang upon my richest robes
  And show itself, attire me how I can.
  Go, lead the way; I long to see my prison. Exeunt

ACT III. SCENE I. The Abbey at Bury St. Edmunds

Sound a sennet. Enter the KING, the QUEEN, CARDINAL,
SUFFOLK, YORK,
BUCKINGHAM, SALISBURY, and WARWICK, to the Parliament

KING HENRY. I muse my Lord of Gloucester is not come.
  'Tis not his wont to be the hindmost man,
  Whate'er occasion keeps him from us now.
QUEEN. Can you not see, or will ye not observe
  The strangeness of his alter'd countenance?
  With what a majesty he bears himself;
  How insolent of late he is become,
  How proud, how peremptory, and unlike himself?
  We know the time since he was mild and affable,
  And if we did but glance a far-off look
  Immediately he was upon his knee,
  That all the court admir'd him for submission.
  But meet him now and be it in the morn,
  When every one will give the time of day,
  He knits his brow and shows an angry eye
  And passeth by with stiff unbowed knee,
  Disdaining duty that to us belongs.
  Small curs are not regarded when they grin,
  But great men tremble when the lion roars,
  And Humphrey is no little man in England.
  First note that he is near you in descent,
  And should you fall he is the next will mount;

42

Me seemeth, then, it is no policy-
Respecting what a rancorous mind he bears,
And his advantage following your decease-
That he should come about your royal person
Or be admitted to your Highness' Council.
By flattery hath he won the commons' hearts;
And when he please to make commotion,
'Tis to be fear'd they all will follow him.
Now 'tis the spring, and weeds are shallow-rooted;
Suffer them now, and they'll o'ergrow the garden
And choke the herbs for want of husbandry.
The reverent care I bear unto my lord
Made me collect these dangers in the Duke.
If it be fond, can it a woman's fear;
Which fear if better reasons can supplant,
I will subscribe, and say I wrong'd the Duke.
My Lord of Suffolk, Buckingham, and York,
Reprove my allegation if you can,
Or else conclude my words effectual.
SUFFOLK. Well hath your Highness seen into this duke;
  And had I first been put to speak my mind,
  I think I should have told your Grace's tale.
  The Duchess, by his subornation,
  Upon my life, began her devilish practices;
  Or if he were not privy to those faults,
  Yet by reputing of his high descent-
  As next the King he was successive heir-
  And such high vaunts of his nobility,
  Did instigate the bedlam brainsick Duchess
  By wicked means to frame our sovereign's fall.
  Smooth runs the water where the brook is deep,
  And in his simple show he harbours treason.
  The fox barks not when he would steal the lamb.
  No, no, my sovereign, Gloucester is a man
  Unsounded yet, and full of deep deceit.
CARDINAL. Did he not, contrary to form of law,
  Devise strange deaths for small offences done?
YORK. And did he not, in his protectorship,
  Levy great sums of money through the realm

For soldiers' pay in France, and never sent it?
By means whereof the towns each day revolted.
BUCKINGHAM. Tut, these are petty faults to faults unknown
Which time will bring to light in smooth Duke Humphrey.
KING HENRY. My lords, at once: the care you have of us,
To mow down thorns that would annoy our foot,
Is worthy praise; but shall I speak my conscience?
Our kinsman Gloucester is as innocent
From meaning treason to our royal person
As is the sucking lamb or harmless dove:
The Duke is virtuous, mild, and too well given
To dream on evil or to work my downfall.
QUEEN. Ah, what's more dangerous than this fond affiance?
Seems he a dove? His feathers are but borrow'd,
For he's disposed as the hateful raven.
Is he a lamb? His skin is surely lent him,
For he's inclin'd as is the ravenous wolf.
Who cannot steal a shape that means deceit?
Take heed, my lord; the welfare of us all
Hangs on the cutting short that fraudful man.

Enter SOMERSET

SOMERSET. All health unto my gracious sovereign!
KING HENRY. Welcome, Lord Somerset. What news from
France?
SOMERSET. That all your interest in those territories
Is utterly bereft you; all is lost.
KING HENRY. Cold news, Lord Somerset; but God's will be
done!
YORK. [Aside] Cold news for me; for I had hope of France
As firmly as I hope for fertile England.
Thus are my blossoms blasted in the bud,
And caterpillars eat my leaves away;
But I will remedy this gear ere long,
Or sell my title for a glorious grave.

Enter GLOUCESTER

44

GLOUCESTER. All happiness unto my lord the King!
  Pardon, my liege, that I have stay'd so long.
SUFFOLK. Nay, Gloucester, know that thou art come too soon,
  Unless thou wert more loyal than thou art.
  I do arrest thee of high treason here.
GLOUCESTER. Well, Suffolk, thou shalt not see me blush
  Nor change my countenance for this arrest:
  A heart unspotted is not easily daunted.
  The purest spring is not so free from mud
  As I am clear from treason to my sovereign.
  Who can accuse me? Wherein am I guilty?
YORK. 'Tis thought, my lord, that you took bribes of France
  And, being Protector, stay'd the soldiers' pay;
  By means whereof his Highness hath lost France.
GLOUCESTER. Is it but thought so? What are they that think it?
  I never robb'd the soldiers of their pay
  Nor ever had one penny bribe from France.
  So help me God, as I have watch'd the night-
  Ay, night by night- in studying good for England!
  That doit that e'er I wrested from the King,
  Or any groat I hoarded to my use,
  Be brought against me at my trial-day!
  No; many a pound of mine own proper store,
  Because I would not tax the needy commons,
  Have I dispursed to the garrisons,
  And never ask'd for restitution.
CARDINAL. It serves you well, my lord, to say so much.
GLOUCESTER. I say no more than truth, so help me God!
YORK. In your protectorship you did devise
  Strange tortures for offenders, never heard of,
  That England was defam'd by tyranny.
GLOUCESTER. Why, 'tis well known that whiles I was Protector
  Pity was all the fault that was in me;
  For I should melt at an offender's tears,
  And lowly words were ransom for their fault.
  Unless it were a bloody murderer,
  Or foul felonious thief that fleec'd poor passengers,
  I never gave them condign punishment.
  Murder indeed, that bloody sin, I tortur'd

45

Above the felon or what trespass else.
SUFFOLK. My lord, these faults are easy, quickly answer'd;
  But mightier crimes are laid unto your charge,
  Whereof you cannot easily purge yourself.
  I do arrest you in His Highness' name,
  And here commit you to my Lord Cardinal
  To keep until your further time of trial.
KING HENRY. My Lord of Gloucester, 'tis my special hope
  That you will clear yourself from all suspense.
  My conscience tells me you are innocent.
GLOUCESTER. Ah, gracious lord, these days are dangerous!
  Virtue is chok'd with foul ambition,
  And charity chas'd hence by rancour's hand;
  Foul subornation is predominant,
  And equity exil'd your Highness' land.
  I know their complot is to have my life;
  And if my death might make this island happy
  And prove the period of their tyranny,
  I would expend it with all willingness.
  But mine is made the prologue to their play;
  For thousands more that yet suspect no peril
  Will not conclude their plotted tragedy.
  Beaufort's red sparkling eyes blab his heart's malice,
  And Suffolk's cloudy brow his stormy hate;
  Sharp Buckingham unburdens with his tongue
  The envious load that lies upon his heart;
  And dogged York, that reaches at the moon,
  Whose overweening arm I have pluck'd back,
  By false accuse doth level at my life.
  And you, my sovereign lady, with the rest,
  Causeless have laid disgraces on my head,
  And with your best endeavour have stirr'd up
  My liefest liege to be mine enemy;
  Ay, all of you have laid your heads together-
  Myself had notice of your conventicles-
  And all to make away my guiltless life.
  I shall not want false witness to condemn me
  Nor store of treasons to augment my guilt.
  The ancient proverb will be well effected:

'A staff is quickly found to beat a dog.'
CARDINAL. My liege, his railing is intolerable.
  If those that care to keep your royal person
  From treason's secret knife and traitor's rage
  Be thus upbraided, chid, and rated at,
  And the offender granted scope of speech,
  'Twill make them cool in zeal unto your Grace.
SUFFOLK. Hath he not twit our sovereign lady here
  With ignominious words, though clerkly couch'd,
  As if she had suborned some to swear
  False allegations to o'erthrow his state?
QUEEN. But I can give the loser leave to chide.
GLOUCESTER. Far truer spoke than meant: I lose indeed.
  Beshrew the winners, for they play'd me false!
  And well such losers may have leave to speak.
BUCKINGHAM. He'll wrest the sense, and hold us here all day.
  Lord Cardinal, he is your prisoner.
CARDINAL. Sirs, take away the Duke, and guard him sure.
GLOUCESTER. Ah, thus King Henry throws away his crutch
  Before his legs be firm to bear his body!
  Thus is the shepherd beaten from thy side,
  And wolves are gnarling who shall gnaw thee first.
  Ah, that my fear were false! ah, that it were!
  For, good King Henry, thy decay I fear. Exit, guarded
KING HENRY. My lords, what to your wisdoms seemeth best
  Do or undo, as if ourself were here.
QUEEN. What, will your Highness leave the Parliament?
KING HENRY. Ay, Margaret; my heart is drown'd with grief,
  Whose flood begins to flow within mine eyes;
  My body round engirt with misery-
  For what's more miserable than discontent?
  Ah, uncle Humphrey, in thy face I see
  The map of honour, truth, and loyalty!
  And yet, good Humphrey, is the hour to come
  That e'er I prov'd thee false or fear'd thy faith.
  What louring star now envies thy estate
  That these great lords, and Margaret our Queen,
  Do seek subversion of thy harmless life?
  Thou never didst them wrong, nor no man wrong;

47

And as the butcher takes away the calf,
And binds the wretch, and beats it when it strays,
Bearing it to the bloody slaughter-house,
Even so, remorseless, have they borne him hence;
And as the dam runs lowing up and down,
Looking the way her harmless young one went,
And can do nought but wail her darling's loss,
Even so myself bewails good Gloucester's case
With sad unhelpful tears, and with dimm'd eyes
Look after him, and cannot do him good,
So mighty are his vowed enemies.
His fortunes I will weep, and 'twixt each groan
Say 'Who's a traitor? Gloucester he is none.' Exit
QUEEN. Free lords, cold snow melts with the sun's hot beams:
  Henry my lord is cold in great affairs,
  Too full of foolish pity; and Gloucester's show
  Beguiles him as the mournful crocodile
  With sorrow snares relenting passengers;
  Or as the snake, roll'd in a flow'ring bank,
  With shining checker'd slough, doth sting a child
  That for the beauty thinks it excellent.
  Believe me, lords, were none more wise than I-
  And yet herein I judge mine own wit good-
  This Gloucester should be quickly rid the world
  To rid us from the fear we have of him.
CARDINAL. That he should die is worthy policy;
  But yet we want a colour for his death.
  'Tis meet he be condemn'd by course of law.
SUFFOLK. But, in my mind, that were no policy:
  The King will labour still to save his life;
  The commons haply rise to save his life;
  And yet we have but trivial argument,
  More than mistrust, that shows him worthy death.
YORK. So that, by this, you would not have him die.
SUFFOLK. Ah, York, no man alive so fain as I!
YORK. 'Tis York that hath more reason for his death.
  But, my Lord Cardinal, and you, my Lord of Suffolk,
  Say as you think, and speak it from your souls:
  Were't not all one an empty eagle were set

To guard the chicken from a hungry kite
As place Duke Humphrey for the King's Protector?
QUEEN. So the poor chicken should be sure of death.
SUFFOLK. Madam, 'tis true; and were't not madness then
To make the fox surveyor of the fold?
Who being accus'd a crafty murderer,
His guilt should be but idly posted over,
Because his purpose is not executed.
No; let him die, in that he is a fox,
By nature prov'd an enemy to the flock,
Before his chaps be stain'd with crimson blood,
As Humphrey, prov'd by reasons, to my liege.
And do not stand on quillets how to slay him;
Be it by gins, by snares, by subtlety,
Sleeping or waking, 'tis no matter how,
So he be dead; for that is good deceit
Which mates him first that first intends deceit.
QUEEN. Thrice-noble Suffolk, 'tis resolutely spoke.
SUFFOLK. Not resolute, except so much were done,
For things are often spoke and seldom meant;
But that my heart accordeth with my tongue,
Seeing the deed is meritorious,
And to preserve my sovereign from his foe,
Say but the word, and I will be his priest.
CARDINAL. But I would have him dead, my Lord of Suffolk,
Ere you can take due orders for a priest;
Say you consent and censure well the deed,
And I'll provide his executioner-
I tender so the safety of my liege.
SUFFOLK. Here is my hand the deed is worthy doing.
QUEEN. And so say I.
YORK. And I. And now we three have spoke it,
It skills not greatly who impugns our doom.

Enter a POST

POST. Great lords, from Ireland am I come amain
To signify that rebels there are up
And put the Englishmen unto the sword.

Send succours, lords, and stop the rage betime,
  Before the wound do grow uncurable;
  For, being green, there is great hope of help.
CARDINAL. A breach that craves a quick expedient stop!
  What counsel give you in this weighty cause?
YORK. That Somerset be sent as Regent thither;
  'Tis meet that lucky ruler be employ'd,
  Witness the fortune he hath had in France.
SOMERSET. If York, with all his far-fet policy,
  Had been the Regent there instead of me,
  He never would have stay'd in France so long.
YORK. No, not to lose it all as thou hast done.
  I rather would have lost my life betimes
  Than bring a burden of dishonour home
  By staying there so long till all were lost.
  Show me one scar character'd on thy skin:
  Men's flesh preserv'd so whole do seldom win.
QUEEN. Nay then, this spark will prove a raging fire,
  If wind and fuel be brought to feed it with;
  No more, good York; sweet Somerset, be still.
  Thy fortune, York, hadst thou been Regent there,
  Might happily have prov'd far worse than his.
YORK. What, worse than nought? Nay, then a shame take all!
SOMERSET. And in the number, thee that wishest shame!
CARDINAL. My Lord of York, try what your fortune is.
  Th' uncivil kerns of Ireland are in arms
  And temper clay with blood of Englishmen;
  To Ireland will you lead a band of men,
  Collected choicely, from each county some,
  And try your hap against the Irishmen?
YORK. I will, my lord, so please his Majesty.
SUFFOLK. Why, our authority is his consent,
  And what we do establish he confirms;
  Then, noble York, take thou this task in hand.
YORK. I am content; provide me soldiers, lords,
  Whiles I take order for mine own affairs.
SUFFOLK. A charge, Lord York, that I will see perform'd.
  But now return we to the false Duke Humphrey.
CARDINAL. No more of him; for I will deal with him

50

That henceforth he shall trouble us no more.
And so break off; the day is almost spent.
Lord Suffolk, you and I must talk of that event.
YORK. My Lord of Suffolk, within fourteen days
  At Bristol I expect my soldiers;
  For there I'll ship them all for Ireland.
SUFFOLK. I'll see it truly done, my Lord of York.
                    Exeunt all but YORK
YORK. Now, York, or never, steel thy fearful thoughts
  And change misdoubt to resolution;
  Be that thou hop'st to be; or what thou art
  Resign to death- it is not worth th' enjoying.
  Let pale-fac'd fear keep with the mean-born man
  And find no harbour in a royal heart.
  Faster than spring-time show'rs comes thought on thought,
  And not a thought but thinks on dignity.
  My brain, more busy than the labouring spider,
  Weaves tedious snares to trap mine enemies.
  Well, nobles, well, 'tis politicly done
  To send me packing with an host of men.
  I fear me you but warm the starved snake,
  Who, cherish'd in your breasts, will sting your hearts.
  'Twas men I lack'd, and you will give them me;
  I take it kindly. Yet be well assur'd
  You put sharp weapons in a madman's hands.
  Whiles I in Ireland nourish a mighty band,
  I will stir up in England some black storm
  Shall blow ten thousand souls to heaven or hell;
  And this fell tempest shall not cease to rage
  Until the golden circuit on my head,
  Like to the glorious sun's transparent beams,
  Do calm the fury of this mad-bred flaw.
  And for a minister of my intent
  I have seduc'd a headstrong Kentishman,
  John Cade of Ashford,
  To make commotion, as full well he can,
  Under the tide of John Mortimer.
  In Ireland have I seen this stubborn Cade
  Oppose himself against a troop of kerns,

And fought so long tiff that his thighs with darts
Were almost like a sharp-quill'd porpentine;
And in the end being rescu'd, I have seen
Him caper upright like a wild Morisco,
Shaking the bloody darts as he his bells.
Full often, like a shag-hair'd crafty kern,
Hath he conversed with the enemy,
And undiscover'd come to me again
And given me notice of their villainies.
This devil here shall be my substitute;
For that John Mortimer, which now is dead,
In face, in gait, in speech, he doth resemble.
By this I shall perceive the commons' mind,
How they affect the house and claim of York.
Say he be taken, rack'd, and tortured;
I know no pain they can inflict upon him
Will make him say I mov'd him to those arms.
Say that he thrive, as 'tis great like he will,
Why, then from Ireland come I with my strength,
And reap the harvest which that rascal sow'd;
For Humphrey being dead, as he shall be,
And Henry put apart, the next for me. Exit

SCENE II. Bury St. Edmunds. A room of state

Enter two or three MURDERERS running over the stage, from the murder of DUKE HUMPHREY

  FIRST MURDERER. Run to my Lord of Suffolk; let him know
    We have dispatch'd the Duke, as he commanded.
  SECOND MURDERER. O that it were to do! What have we done?
    Didst ever hear a man so penitent?

Enter SUFFOLK

FIRST MURDERER. Here comes my lord.
SUFFOLK. Now, sirs, have you dispatch'd this thing?
FIRST MURDERER. Ay, my good lord, he's dead.
SUFFOLK. Why, that's well said. Go, get you to my house;
  I will reward you for this venturous deed.
  The King and all the peers are here at hand.
  Have you laid fair the bed? Is all things well,
  According as I gave directions?
FIRST MURDERER. 'Tis, my good lord.
SUFFOLK. Away! be gone. Exeunt MURDERERS

Sound trumpets. Enter the KING, the QUEEN,
CARDINAL, SOMERSET, with attendants

KING HENRY. Go call our uncle to our presence straight;
  Say we intend to try his Grace to-day,
  If he be guilty, as 'tis published.
SUFFOLK. I'll call him presently, my noble lord. Exit
KING HENRY. Lords, take your places; and, I pray you all,
  Proceed no straiter 'gainst our uncle Gloucester
  Than from true evidence, of good esteem,
  He be approv'd in practice culpable.
QUEEN. God forbid any malice should prevail
  That faultless may condemn a nobleman!
  Pray God he may acquit him of suspicion!
KING HENRY. I thank thee, Meg; these words content me much.

Re-enter SUFFOLK

How now! Why look'st thou pale? Why tremblest thou?
  Where is our uncle? What's the matter, Suffolk?
SUFFOLK. Dead in his bed, my lord; Gloucester is dead.
QUEEN. Marry, God forfend!
CARDINAL. God's secret judgment! I did dream to-night
  The Duke was dumb and could not speak a word.
                    [The KING swoons]
QUEEN. How fares my lord? Help, lords! The King is dead.
SOMERSET. Rear up his body; wring him by the nose.
QUEEN. Run, go, help, help! O Henry, ope thine eyes!
SUFFOLK. He doth revive again; madam, be patient.

KING. O heavenly God!

QUEEN. How fares my gracious lord?

SUFFOLK. Comfort, my sovereign! Gracious Henry, comfort!

KING HENRY. What, doth my Lord of Suffolk comfort me?
  Came he right now to sing a raven's note,
  Whose dismal tune bereft my vital pow'rs;
  And thinks he that the chirping of a wren,
  By crying comfort from a hollow breast,
  Can chase away the first conceived sound?
  Hide not thy poison with such sug'red words;
  Lay not thy hands on me; forbear, I say,
  Their touch affrights me as a serpent's sting.
  Thou baleful messenger, out of my sight!
  Upon thy eye-balls murderous tyranny
  Sits in grim majesty to fright the world.
  Look not upon me, for thine eyes are wounding;
  Yet do not go away; come, basilisk,
  And kill the innocent gazer with thy sight;
  For in the shade of death I shall find joy-
  In life but double death,'now Gloucester's dead.

QUEEN. Why do you rate my Lord of Suffolk thus?
  Although the Duke was enemy to him,
  Yet he most Christian-like laments his death;
  And for myself- foe as he was to me-
  Might liquid tears, or heart-offending groans,
  Or blood-consuming sighs, recall his life,
  I would be blind with weeping, sick with groans,
  Look pale as primrose with blood-drinking sighs,
  And all to have the noble Duke alive.
  What know I how the world may deem of me?
  For it is known we were but hollow friends:
  It may be judg'd I made the Duke away;
  So shall my name with slander's tongue be wounded,
  And princes' courts be fill'd with my reproach.
  This get I by his death. Ay me, unhappy!
  To be a queen and crown'd with infamy!

KING HENRY. Ah, woe is me for Gloucester, wretched man!

QUEEN. Be woe for me, more wretched than he is.
  What, dost thou turn away, and hide thy face?

I am no loathsome leper- look on me.
What, art thou like the adder waxen deaf?
Be poisonous too, and kill thy forlorn Queen.
Is all thy comfort shut in Gloucester's tomb?
Why, then Dame Margaret was ne'er thy joy.
Erect his statue and worship it,
And make my image but an alehouse sign.
Was I for this nigh wreck'd upon the sea,
And twice by awkward wind from England's bank
Drove back again unto my native clime?
What boded this but well-forewarning wind
Did seem to say 'Seek not a scorpion's nest,
Nor set no footing on this unkind shore'?
What did I then but curs'd the gentle gusts,
And he that loos'd them forth their brazen caves;
And bid them blow towards England's blessed shore,
Or turn our stern upon a dreadful rock?
Yet Aeolus would not be a murderer,
But left that hateful office unto thee.
The pretty-vaulting sea refus'd to drown me,
Knowing that thou wouldst have me drown'd on shore
With tears as salt as sea through thy unkindness;
The splitting rocks cow'r'd in the sinking sands
And would not dash me with their ragged sides,
Because thy flinty heart, more hard than they,
Might in thy palace perish Margaret.
As far as I could ken thy chalky cliffs,
When from thy shore the tempest beat us back,
I stood upon the hatches in the storm;
And when the dusky sky began to rob
My earnest-gaping sight of thy land's view,
I took a costly jewel from my neck-
A heart it was, bound in with diamonds-
And threw it towards thy land. The sea receiv'd it;
And so I wish'd thy body might my heart.
And even with this I lost fair England's view,
And bid mine eyes be packing with my heart,
And call'd them blind and dusky spectacles
For losing ken of Albion's wished coast.

How often have I tempted Suffolk's tongue-
The agent of thy foul inconstancy-
To sit and witch me, as Ascanius did
When he to madding Dido would unfold
His father's acts commenc'd in burning Troy!
Am I not witch'd like her? Or thou not false like him?
Ay me, I can no more! Die, Margaret,
For Henry weeps that thou dost live so long.

Noise within. Enter WARWICK, SALISBURY,
and many commons

WARWICK. It is reported, mighty sovereign,
  That good Duke Humphrey traitorously is murd'red
  By Suffolk and the Cardinal Beaufort's means.
  The commons, like an angry hive of bees
  That want their leader, scatter up and down
  And care not who they sting in his revenge.
  Myself have calm'd their spleenful mutiny
  Until they hear the order of his death.
KING HENRY. That he is dead, good Warwick, 'tis too true;
  But how he died God knows, not Henry.
  Enter his chamber, view his breathless corpse,
  And comment then upon his sudden death.
WARWICK. That shall I do, my liege. Stay, Salisbury,
  With the rude multitude till I return. *Exit*
                    Exit SALISBURY with the commons
KING HENRY. O Thou that judgest all things, stay my thoughts-
  My thoughts that labour to persuade my soul
  Some violent hands were laid on Humphrey's life!
  If my suspect be false, forgive me, God;
  For judgment only doth belong to Thee.
  Fain would I go to chafe his paly lips
  With twenty thousand kisses and to drain
  Upon his face an ocean of salt tears
  To tell my love unto his dumb deaf trunk;
  And with my fingers feel his hand un-feeling;
  But all in vain are these mean obsequies;

And to survey his dead and earthy image,
What were it but to make my sorrow greater?

Bed put forth with the body. Enter WARWICK

WARWICK. Come hither, gracious sovereign, view this body.
KING HENRY. That is to see how deep my grave is made;
  For with his soul fled all my worldly solace,
  For, seeing him, I see my life in death.
WARWICK. As surely as my soul intends to live
  With that dread King that took our state upon Him
  To free us from his Father's wrathful curse,
  I do believe that violent hands were laid
  Upon the life of this thrice-famed Duke.
SUFFOLK. A dreadful oath, sworn with a solemn tongue!
  What instance gives Lord Warwick for his vow?
WARWICK. See how the blood is settled in his face.
  Oft have I seen a timely-parted ghost,
  Of ashy semblance, meagre, pale, and bloodless,
  Being all descended to the labouring heart,
  Who, in the conflict that it holds with death,
  Attracts the same for aidance 'gainst the enemy,
  Which with the heart there cools, and ne'er returneth
  To blush and beautify the cheek again.
  But see, his face is black and full of blood;
  His eye-balls further out than when he liv'd,
  Staring full ghastly like a strangled man;
  His hair uprear'd, his nostrils stretch'd with struggling;
  His hands abroad display'd, as one that grasp'd
  And tugg'd for life, and was by strength subdu'd.
  Look, on the sheets his hair, you see, is sticking;
  His well-proportion'd beard made rough and rugged,
  Like to the summer's corn by tempest lodged.
  It cannot be but he was murd'red here:
  The least of all these signs were probable.
SUFFOLK. Why, Warwick, who should do the Duke to death?
  Myself and Beaufort had him in protection;
  And we, I hope, sir, are no murderers.
WARWICK. But both of you were vow'd Duke Humphrey's foes;

57

And you, forsooth, had the good Duke to keep.
'Tis like you would not feast him like a friend;
And 'tis well seen he found an enemy.
QUEEN. Then you, belike, suspect these noblemen
  As guilty of Duke Humphrey's timeless death.
WARWICK. Who finds the heifer dead and bleeding fresh,
  And sees fast by a butcher with an axe,
  But will suspect 'twas he that made the slaughter?
  Who finds the partridge in the puttock's nest
  But may imagine how the bird was dead,
  Although the kite soar with unbloodied beak?
  Even so suspicious is this tragedy.
QUEEN. Are you the butcher, Suffolk? Where's your knife?
  Is Beaufort term'd a kite? Where are his talons?
SUFFOLK. I wear no knife to slaughter sleeping men;
  But here's a vengeful sword, rusted with ease,
  That shall be scoured in his rancorous heart
  That slanders me with murder's crimson badge.
  Say if thou dar'st, proud Lord of Warwickshire,
  That I am faulty in Duke Humphrey's death.
                    Exeunt CARDINAL, SOMERSET, and others
WARWICK. What dares not Warwick, if false Suffolk dare him?
QUEEN. He dares not calm his contumelious spirit,
  Nor cease to be an arrogant controller,
  Though Suffolk dare him twenty thousand times.
WARWICK. Madam, be still- with reverence may I say;
  For every word you speak in his behalf
  Is slander to your royal dignity.
SUFFOLK. Blunt-witted lord, ignoble in demeanour,
  If ever lady wrong'd her lord so much,
  Thy mother took into her blameful bed
  Some stern untutor'd churl, and noble stock
  Was graft with crab-tree slip, whose fruit thou art,
  And never of the Nevils' noble race.
WARWICK. But that the guilt of murder bucklers thee,
  And I should rob the deathsman of his fee,
  Quitting thee thereby of ten thousand shames,
  And that my sovereign's presence makes me mild,
  I would, false murd'rous coward, on thy knee

Make thee beg pardon for thy passed speech
And say it was thy mother that thou meant'st,
That thou thyself was born in bastardy;
And, after all this fearful homage done,
Give thee thy hire and send thy soul to hell,
Pernicious blood-sucker of sleeping men.
SUFFOLK. Thou shalt be waking while I shed thy blood,
If from this presence thou dar'st go with me.
WARWICK. Away even now, or I will drag thee hence.
Unworthy though thou art, I'll cope with thee,
And do some service to Duke Humphrey's ghost.
                    Exeunt SUFFOLK and WARWICK
KING HENRY. What stronger breastplate than a heart untainted?
Thrice is he arm'd that hath his quarrel just;
And he but naked, though lock'd up in steel,
Whose conscience with injustice is corrupted.
                    [A noise within]
QUEEN. What noise is this?

Re-enter SUFFOLK and WARWICK, with their weapons drawn

KING. Why, how now, lords, your wrathful weapons drawn
Here in our presence! Dare you be so bold?
Why, what tumultuous clamour have we here?
SUFFOLK. The trait'rous Warwick, with the men of Bury,
Set all upon me, mighty sovereign.

Re-enter SALISBURY

SALISBURY. [To the Commons within] Sirs, stand apart, the King
shall know your mind.
Dread lord, the commons send you word by me
Unless Lord Suffolk straight be done to death,
Or banished fair England's territories,
They will by violence tear him from your palace
And torture him with grievous ling'ring death.
They say by him the good Duke Humphrey died;
They say in him they fear your Highness' death;
And mere instinct of love and loyalty,
Free from a stubborn opposite intent,

59

As being thought to contradict your liking,
Makes them thus forward in his banishment.
They say, in care of your most royal person,
That if your Highness should intend to sleep
And charge that no man should disturb your rest,
In pain of your dislike or pain of death,
Yet, notwithstanding such a strait edict,
Were there a serpent seen with forked tongue
That slily glided towards your Majesty,
It were but necessary you were wak'd,
Lest, being suffer'd in that harmful slumber,
The mortal worm might make the sleep eternal.
And therefore do they cry, though you forbid,
That they will guard you, whe'er you will or no,
From such fell serpents as false Suffolk is;
With whose envenomed and fatal sting
Your loving uncle, twenty times his worth,
They say, is shamefully bereft of life.

COMMONS. [Within] An answer from the King, my Lord of
Salisbury!

SUFFOLK. 'Tis like the commons, rude unpolish'd hinds,
Could send such message to their sovereign;
But you, my lord, were glad to be employ'd,
To show how quaint an orator you are.
But all the honour Salisbury hath won
Is that he was the lord ambassador
Sent from a sort of tinkers to the King.

COMMONS. [Within] An answer from the King, or we will all
break in!

KING HENRY. Go, Salisbury, and tell them all from me
I thank them for their tender loving care;
And had I not been cited so by them,
Yet did I purpose as they do entreat;
For sure my thoughts do hourly prophesy
Mischance unto my state by Suffolk's means.
And therefore by His Majesty I swear,
Whose far unworthy deputy I am,
He shall not breathe infection in this air
But three days longer, on the pain of death.

60

QUEEN. O Henry, let me plead for gentle Suffolk!

KING HENRY. Ungentle Queen, to call him gentle Suffolk!
  No more, I say; if thou dost plead for him,
  Thou wilt but add increase unto my wrath.
  Had I but said, I would have kept my word;
  But when I swear, it is irrevocable.
  If after three days' space thou here be'st found
  On any ground that I am ruler of,
  The world shall not be ransom for thy life.
  Come, Warwick, come, good Warwick, go with me;
  I have great matters to impart to thee.
                    Exeunt all but QUEEN and SUFFOLK
QUEEN. Mischance and sorrow go along with you!
  Heart's discontent and sour affliction
  Be playfellows to keep you company!
  There's two of you; the devil make a third,
  And threefold vengeance tend upon your steps!

SUFFOLK. Cease, gentle Queen, these execrations,
  And let thy Suffolk take his heavy leave.

QUEEN. Fie, coward woman and soft-hearted wretch,
  Has thou not spirit to curse thine enemy?

SUFFOLK. A plague upon them! Wherefore should I curse them?
  Would curses kill as doth the mandrake's groan,
  I would invent as bitter searching terms,
  As curst, as harsh, and horrible to hear,
  Deliver'd strongly through my fixed teeth,
  With full as many signs of deadly hate,
  As lean-fac'd Envy in her loathsome cave.
  My tongue should stumble in mine earnest words,
  Mine eyes should sparkle like the beaten flint,
  Mine hair be fix'd an end, as one distract;
  Ay, every joint should seem to curse and ban;
  And even now my burden'd heart would break,
  Should I not curse them. Poison be their drink!
  Gall, worse than gall, the daintiest that they taste!
  Their sweetest shade a grove of cypress trees!
  Their chiefest prospect murd'ring basilisks!
  Their softest touch as smart as lizards' stings!

Their music frightful as the serpent's hiss,
And boding screech-owls make the consort full!
all the foul terrors in dark-seated hell-
QUEEN. Enough, sweet Suffolk, thou torment'st thyself;
  And these dread curses, like the sun 'gainst glass,
  Or like an overcharged gun, recoil,
  And turns the force of them upon thyself.
SUFFOLK. You bade me ban, and will you bid me leave?
  Now, by the ground that I am banish'd from,
  Well could I curse away a winter's night,
  Though standing naked on a mountain top
  Where biting cold would never let grass grow,
  And think it but a minute spent in sport.
QUEEN. O, let me entreat thee cease! Give me thy hand,
  That I may dew it with my mournful tears;
  Nor let the rain of heaven wet this place
  To wash away my woeful monuments.
  O, could this kiss be printed in thy hand,
  That thou might'st think upon these by the seal,
  Through whom a thousand sighs are breath'd for thee!
  So, get thee gone, that I may know my grief;
  'Tis but surmis'd whiles thou art standing by,
  As one that surfeits thinking on a want.
  I will repeal thee or, be well assur'd,
  Adventure to be banished myself;
  And banished I am, if but from thee.
  Go, speak not to me; even now be gone.
  O, go not yet! Even thus two friends condemn'd
  Embrace, and kiss, and take ten thousand leaves,
  Loather a hundred times to part than die.
  Yet now, farewell; and farewell life with thee!
SUFFOLK. Thus is poor Suffolk ten times banished,
  Once by the King and three times thrice by thee,
  'Tis not the land I care for, wert thou thence;
  A wilderness is populous enough,
  So Suffolk had thy heavenly company;
  For where thou art, there is the world itself,
  With every several pleasure in the world;
  And where thou art not, desolation.

I can no more: Live thou to joy thy life;
Myself no joy in nought but that thou liv'st.

Enter VAUX

QUEEN. Whither goes Vaux so fast? What news, I prithee?
VAUX. To signify unto his Majesty
    That Cardinal Beaufort is at point of death;
    For suddenly a grievous sickness took him
    That makes him gasp, and stare, and catch the air,
    Blaspheming God, and cursing men on earth.
    Sometime he talks as if Duke Humphrey's ghost
    Were by his side; sometime he calls the King
    And whispers to his pillow, as to him,
    The secrets of his overcharged soul;
    And I am sent to tell his Majesty
    That even now he cries aloud for him.
QUEEN. Go tell this heavy message to the King. Exit VAUX
    Ay me! What is this world! What news are these!
    But wherefore grieve I at an hour's poor loss,
    Omitting Suffolk's exile, my soul's treasure?
    Why only, Suffolk, mourn I not for thee,
    And with the southern clouds contend in tears-
    Theirs for the earth's increase, mine for my sorrows?
    Now get thee hence: the King, thou know'st, is coming;
    If thou be found by me; thou art but dead.
SUFFOLK. If I depart from thee I cannot live;
    And in thy sight to die, what were it else
    But like a pleasant slumber in thy lap?
    Here could I breathe my soul into the air,
    As mild and gentle as the cradle-babe
    Dying with mother's dug between its lips;
    Where, from thy sight, I should be raging mad
    And cry out for thee to close up mine eyes,
    To have thee with thy lips to stop my mouth;
    So shouldst thou either turn my flying soul,
    Or I should breathe it so into thy body,
    And then it liv'd in sweet Elysium.
    To die by thee were but to die in jest:

63

From thee to die were torture more than death.
O, let me stay, befall what may befall!
QUEEN. Away! Though parting be a fretful corrosive,
  It is applied to a deathful wound.
  To France, sweet Suffolk. Let me hear from thee;
  For whereso'er thou art in this world's globe
  I'll have an Iris that shall find thee out.
SUFFOLK. I go.
QUEEN. And take my heart with thee. [She kisses him]
SUFFOLK. A jewel, lock'd into the woefull'st cask
  That ever did contain a thing of worth.
  Even as a splitted bark, so sunder we:
  This way fall I to death.
QUEEN. This way for me. Exeunt severally

SCENE III. London. CARDINAL BEAUFORT'S bedchamber

Enter the KING, SALISBURY, and WARWICK, to the
CARDINAL in bed

  KING HENRY. How fares my lord? Speak, Beaufort, to thy
sovereign.
  CARDINAL. If thou be'st Death I'll give thee England's treasure,
  Enough to purchase such another island,
  So thou wilt let me live and feel no pain.
  KING HENRY. Ah, what a sign it is of evil life
  Where death's approach is seen so terrible!
  WARWICK. Beaufort, it is thy sovereign speaks to thee.
  CARDINAL. Bring me unto my trial when you will.
  Died he not in his bed? Where should he die?
  Can I make men live, whe'er they will or no?
  O, torture me no more! I will confess.
  Alive again? Then show me where he is;
  I'll give a thousand pound to look upon him.

He hath no eyes, the dust hath blinded them.
Comb down his hair; look, look! it stands upright,
Like lime-twigs set to catch my winged soul!
Give me some drink; and bid the apothecary
Bring the strong poison that I bought of him.
KING HENRY. O Thou eternal Mover of the heavens,
  Look with a gentle eye upon this wretch!
  O, beat away the busy meddling fiend
  That lays strong siege unto this wretch's soul,
  And from his bosom purge this black despair!
WARWICK. See how the pangs of death do make him grin
SALISBURY. Disturb him not, let him pass peaceably.
KING HENRY. Peace to his soul, if God's good pleasure be!
  Lord Card'nal, if thou think'st on heaven's bliss,
  Hold up thy hand, make signal of thy hope.
  He dies, and makes no sign: O God, forgive him!
WARWICK. So bad a death argues a monstrous life.
KING HENRY. Forbear to judge, for we are sinners all.
  Close up his eyes, and draw the curtain close;
  And let us all to meditation. Exeunt

ACT IV. SCENE I. The coast of Kent

Alarum. Fight at sea. Ordnance goes off. Enter a LIEUTENANT, a
SHIPMASTER and his MATE, and WALTER WHITMORE, with
sailors; SUFFOLK and other GENTLEMEN, as prisoners

  LIEUTENANT. The gaudy, blabbing, and remorseful day
    Is crept into the bosom of the sea;
    And now loud-howling wolves arouse the jades
    That drag the tragic melancholy night;
    Who with their drowsy, slow, and flagging wings
    Clip dead men's graves, and from their misty jaws
    Breathe foul contagious darkness in the air.
    Therefore bring forth the soldiers of our prize;
    For, whilst our pinnace anchors in the Downs,
    Here shall they make their ransom on the sand,

Or with their blood stain this discoloured shore.
Master, this prisoner freely give I thee;
And thou that art his mate make boot of this;
The other, Walter Whitmore, is thy share.
FIRST GENTLEMAN. What is my ransom, master, let me know?
MASTER. A thousand crowns, or else lay down your head.
MATE. And so much shall you give, or off goes yours.
LIEUTENANT. What, think you much to pay two thousand crowns,
    And bear the name and port of gentlemen?
    Cut both the villains' throats- for die you shall;
    The lives of those which we have lost in fight
    Be counterpois'd with such a petty sum!
FIRST GENTLEMAN. I'll give it, sir: and therefore spare my life.
SECOND GENTLEMAN. And so will I, and write home for it straight.
WHITMORE. I lost mine eye in laying the prize aboard,
    [To SUFFOLK] And therefore, to revenge it, shalt thou die;
    And so should these, if I might have my will.
LIEUTENANT. Be not so rash; take ransom, let him live.
SUFFOLK. Look on my George, I am a gentleman:
    Rate me at what thou wilt, thou shalt be paid.
WHITMORE. And so am I: my name is Walter Whitmore.
    How now! Why start'st thou? What, doth death affright?
SUFFOLK. Thy name affrights me, in whose sound is death.
    A cunning man did calculate my birth
    And told me that by water I should die;
    Yet let not this make thee be bloody-minded;
    Thy name is Gualtier, being rightly sounded.
WHITMORE. Gualtier or Walter, which it is I care not:
    Never yet did base dishonour blur our name
    But with our sword we wip'd away the blot;
    Therefore, when merchant-like I sell revenge,
    Broke be my sword, my arms torn and defac'd,
    And I proclaim'd a coward through the world.
SUFFOLK. Stay, Whitmore, for thy prisoner is a prince,
    The Duke of Suffolk, William de la Pole.
WHITMORE. The Duke of Suffolk muffled up in rags?
SUFFOLK. Ay, but these rags are no part of the Duke:

Jove sometime went disguis'd, and why not I?

LIEUTENANT. But Jove was never slain, as thou shalt be.

SUFFOLK. Obscure and lowly swain, King Henry's blood,
  The honourable blood of Lancaster,
  Must not be shed by such a jaded groom.
  Hast thou not kiss'd thy hand and held my stirrup,
  Bareheaded plodded by my foot-cloth mule,
  And thought thee happy when I shook my head?
  How often hast thou waited at my cup,
  Fed from my trencher, kneel'd down at the board,
  When I have feasted with Queen Margaret?
  Remember it, and let it make thee crestfall'n,
  Ay, and allay thus thy abortive pride,
  How in our voiding-lobby hast thou stood
  And duly waited for my coming forth.
  This hand of mine hath writ in thy behalf,
  And therefore shall it charm thy riotous tongue.

WHITMORE. Speak, Captain, shall I stab the forlorn swain?

LIEUTENANT. First let my words stab him, as he hath me.

SUFFOLK. Base slave, thy words are blunt, and so art thou.

LIEUTENANT. Convey him hence, and on our longboat's side
  Strike off his head.

SUFFOLK. Thou dar'st not, for thy own.

LIEUTENANT. Poole!

SUFFOLK. Poole?

LIEUTENANT. Ay, kennel, puddle, sink, whose filth and dirt
  Troubles the silver spring where England drinks;
  Now will I dam up this thy yawning mouth
  For swallowing the treasure of the realm.
  Thy lips, that kiss'd the Queen, shall sweep the ground;
  And thou that smil'dst at good Duke Humphrey's death
  Against the senseless winds shalt grin in vain,
  Who in contempt shall hiss at thee again;
  And wedded be thou to the hags of hell
  For daring to affy a mighty lord
  Unto the daughter of a worthless king,
  Having neither subject, wealth, nor diadem.
  By devilish policy art thou grown great,
  And, like ambitious Sylla, overgorg'd

With gobbets of thy mother's bleeding heart.
By thee Anjou and Maine were sold to France;
The false revolting Normans thorough thee
Disdain to call us lord; and Picardy
Hath slain their governors, surpris'd our forts,
And sent the ragged soldiers wounded home.
The princely Warwick, and the Nevils all,
Whose dreadful swords were never drawn in vain,
As hating thee, are rising up in arms;
And now the house of York- thrust from the crown
By shameful murder of a guiltless king
And lofty proud encroaching tyranny-
Burns with revenging fire, whose hopeful colours
Advance our half-fac'd sun, striving to shine,
Under the which is writ 'Invitis nubibus.'
The commons here in Kent are up in arms;
And to conclude, reproach and beggary
Is crept into the palace of our King,
And all by thee. Away! convey him hence.
SUFFOLK. O that I were a god, to shoot forth thunder
  Upon these paltry, servile, abject drudges!
  Small things make base men proud: this villain here,
  Being captain of a pinnace, threatens more
  Than Bargulus, the strong Illyrian pirate.
  Drones suck not eagles' blood but rob beehives.
  It is impossible that I should die
  By such a lowly vassal as thyself.
  Thy words move rage and not remorse in me.
  I go of message from the Queen to France:
  I charge thee waft me safely cross the Channel.
LIEUTENANT. Walter-
WHITMORE. Come, Suffolk, I must waft thee to thy death.
SUFFOLK. Gelidus timor occupat artus: it is thee I fear.
WHITMORE. Thou shalt have cause to fear before I leave thee.
  What, are ye daunted now? Now will ye stoop?
FIRST GENTLEMAN. My gracious lord, entreat him, speak him fair.
SUFFOLK. Suffolk's imperial tongue is stem and rough,
  Us'd to command, untaught to plead for favour.

Far be it we should honour such as these
With humble suit: no, rather let my head
Stoop to the block than these knees bow to any
Save to the God of heaven and to my king;
And sooner dance upon a bloody pole
Than stand uncover'd to the vulgar groom.
True nobility is exempt from fear:
More can I bear than you dare execute.
LIEUTENANT. Hale him away, and let him talk no more.
SUFFOLK. Come, soldiers, show what cruelty ye can,
  That this my death may never be forgot-
  Great men oft die by vile bezonians:
  A Roman sworder and banditto slave
  Murder'd sweet Tully; Brutus' bastard hand
  Stabb'd Julius Caesar; savage islanders
  Pompey the Great; and Suffolk dies by pirates.
                      Exit WALTER with SUFFOLK
LIEUTENANT. And as for these, whose ransom we have set,
  It is our pleasure one of them depart;
  Therefore come you with us, and let him go.
                      Exeunt all but the FIRST GENTLEMAN

Re-enter WHITMORE with SUFFOLK'S body

WHITMORE. There let his head and lifeless body lie,
  Until the Queen his mistress bury it. Exit
FIRST GENTLEMAN. O barbarous and bloody spectacle!
  His body will I bear unto the King.
  If he revenge it not, yet will his friends;
  So will the Queen, that living held him dear.
                      Exit with the body

SCENE II. *Blackheath*

Enter GEORGE BEVIS and JOHN HOLLAND

GEORGE. Come and get thee a sword, though made of a lath; they have

  been up these two days.

JOHN. They have the more need to sleep now, then.

GEORGE. I tell thee Jack Cade the clothier means to dress the
  commonwealth, and turn it, and set a new nap upon it.

JOHN. So he had need, for 'tis threadbare. Well, I say it was never
  merry world in England since gentlemen came up.

GEORGE. O miserable age! Virtue is not regarded in handicraftsmen.

JOHN. The nobility think scorn to go in leather aprons.

GEORGE. Nay, more, the King's Council are no good workmen.

JOHN. True; and yet it is said 'Labour in thy vocation'; which is
  as much to say as 'Let the magistrates be labouring men'; and
  therefore should we be magistrates.

GEORGE. Thou hast hit it; for there's no better sign of a brave
  mind than a hard hand.

JOHN. I see them! I see them! There's Best's son, the tanner of
  Wingham-

GEORGE. He shall have the skins of our enemies to make dog's
  leather of.

JOHN. And Dick the butcher-

GEORGE. Then is sin struck down, like an ox, and iniquity's throat
  cut like a calf.

JOHN. And Smith the weaver-

GEORGE. Argo, their thread of life is spun.

JOHN. Come, come, let's fall in with them.

    Drum. Enter CADE, DICK THE BUTCHER, SMITH
    THE WEAVER, and a SAWYER, with infinite numbers

CADE. We John Cade, so term'd of our supposed father-

DICK. [Aside] Or rather, of stealing a cade of herrings.

CADE. For our enemies shall fall before us, inspired with the
  spirit of putting down kings and princes- command silence.

DICK. Silence!

CADE. My father was a Mortimer-

DICK. [Aside] He was an honest man and a good bricklayer.

CADE. My mother a Plantagenet-

70

DICK. [Aside] I knew her well; she was a midwife.

CADE. My wife descended of the Lacies-

DICK. [Aside] She was, indeed, a pedlar's daughter, and sold many laces.

SMITH. [Aside] But now of late, not able to travel with her furr'd pack, she washes bucks here at home.

CADE. Therefore am I of an honourable house.

DICK. [Aside] Ay, by my faith, the field is honourable, and there was he born, under a hedge, for his father had never a house but the cage.

CADE. Valiant I am.

SMITH. [Aside] 'A must needs; for beggary is valiant.

CADE. I am able to endure much.

DICK. [Aside] No question of that; for I have seen him whipt three market days together.

CADE. I fear neither sword nor fire.

SMITH. [Aside] He need not fear the sword, for his coat is of proof.

DICK. [Aside] But methinks he should stand in fear of fire, being burnt i' th' hand for stealing of sheep.

CADE. Be brave, then, for your captain is brave, and vows reformation. There shall be in England seven halfpenny loaves sold for a penny; the three-hoop'd pot shall have ten hoops; and I will make it felony to drink small beer. All the realm shall be in common, and in Cheapside shall my palfrey go to grass. And when I am king- as king I will be

ALL. God save your Majesty!

CADE. I thank you, good people- there shall be no money; all shall eat and drink on my score, and I will apparel them all in one livery, that they may agree like brothers and worship me their lord.

DICK. The first thing we do, let's kill all the lawyers.

CADE. Nay, that I mean to do. Is not this a lamentable thing, that of the skin of an innocent lamb should be made parchment? That parchment, being scribbl'd o'er, should undo a man? Some say the bee stings; but I say 'tis the bee's wax; for I did but seal once to a thing, and I was never mine own man since. How now! Who's there?

Enter some, bringing in the CLERK OF CHATHAM

SMITH. The clerk of Chatham. He can write and read and cast
  accompt.
CADE. O monstrous!
SMITH. We took him setting of boys' copies.
CADE. Here's a villain!
SMITH. Has a book in his pocket with red letters in't.
CADE. Nay, then he is a conjurer.
DICK. Nay, he can make obligations and write court-hand.
CADE. I am sorry for't; the man is a proper man, of mine honour;
  unless I find him guilty, he shall not die. Come hither, sirrah,
  I must examine thee. What is thy name?
CLERK. Emmanuel.
DICK. They use to write it on the top of letters; 'twill go hard
  with you.
CADE. Let me alone. Dost thou use to write thy name, or hast thou
a
  mark to thyself, like a honest plain-dealing man?
CLERK. Sir, I thank God, I have been so well brought up that I can
  write my name.
ALL. He hath confess'd. Away with him! He's a villain and a
  traitor.
CADE. Away with him, I say! Hang him with his pen and inkhorn
about
  his neck. Exit one with the CLERK

Enter MICHAEL

MICHAEL. Where's our General?
CADE. Here I am, thou particular fellow.
MICHAEL. Fly, fly, fly! Sir Humphrey Stafford and his brother are
  hard by, with the King's forces.
CADE. Stand, villain, stand, or I'll fell thee down. He shall be
  encount'red with a man as good as himself. He is but a knight,
  is 'a?
MICHAEL. No.
CADE. To equal him, I will make myself a knight presently.
  [Kneels] Rise up, Sir John Mortimer. [Rises] Now have at him!

Enter SIR HUMPHREY STAFFORD and WILLIAM
his brother, with drum and soldiers

STAFFORD. Rebellious hinds, the filth and scum of Kent,
  Mark'd for the gallows, lay your weapons down;
  Home to your cottages, forsake this groom;
  The King is merciful if you revolt.
WILLIAM STAFFORD. But angry, wrathful, and inclin'd to blood,
  If you go forward; therefore yield or die.
CADE. As for these silken-coated slaves, I pass not;
  It is to you, good people, that I speak,
  O'er whom, in time to come, I hope to reign;
  For I am rightful heir unto the crown.
STAFFORD. Villain, thy father was a plasterer;
  And thou thyself a shearman, art thou not?
CADE. And Adam was a gardener.
WILLIAM STAFFORD. And what of that?
CADE. Marry, this: Edmund Mortimer, Earl of March,
  Married the Duke of Clarence' daughter, did he not?
STAFFORD. Ay, sir.
CADE. By her he had two children at one birth.
WILLIAM STAFFORD. That's false.
CADE. Ay, there's the question; but I say 'tis true.
  The elder of them being put to nurse,
  Was by a beggar-woman stol'n away,
  And, ignorant of his birth and parentage,
  Became a bricklayer when he came to age.
  His son am I; deny it if you can.
DICK. Nay, 'tis too true; therefore he shall be king.
SMITH. Sir, he made a chimney in my father's house, and the
bricks
  are alive at this day to testify it; therefore deny it not.
STAFFORD. And will you credit this base drudge's words
  That speaks he knows not what?
ALL. Ay, marry, will we; therefore get ye gone.
WILLIAM STAFFORD. Jack Cade, the Duke of York hath taught
you this.
CADE. [Aside] He lies, for I invented it myself- Go to, sirrah,
  tell the King from me that for his father's sake, Henry the

73

Fifth, in whose time boys went to span-counter for French crowns,
I am content he shall reign; but I'll be Protector over him.

DICK. And furthermore, we'll have the Lord Say's head for selling
the dukedom of Maine.

CADE. And good reason; for thereby is England main'd and fain to go
with a staff, but that my puissance holds it up. Fellow kings, I
tell you that that Lord Say hath gelded the commonwealth and made
it an eunuch; and more than that, he can speak French, and
therefore he is a traitor.

STAFFORD. O gross and miserable ignorance!

CADE. Nay, answer if you can; the Frenchmen are our enemies. Go to,
then, I ask but this: can he that speaks with the tongue of an
enemy be a good counsellor, or no?

ALL. No, no; and therefore we'll have his head.

WILLIAM STAFFORD. Well, seeing gentle words will not prevail,
Assail them with the army of the King.

STAFFORD. Herald, away; and throughout every town
Proclaim them traitors that are up with Cade;
That those which fly before the battle ends
May, even in their wives'and children's sight,
Be hang'd up for example at their doors.
And you that be the King's friends, follow me.

      Exeunt the TWO STAFFORDS *and soldiers*

CADE. And you that love the commons follow me.
Now show yourselves men; 'tis for liberty.
We will not leave one lord, one gentleman;
Spare none but such as go in clouted shoon,
For they are thrifty honest men and such
As would- but that they dare not- take our parts.

DICK. They are all in order, and march toward us.

CADE. But then are we in order when we are most out of order. Come,
march forward. *Exeunt*

74

SCENE III. *Another part of Blackheath*

*Alarums to the fight, wherein both the STAFFORDS are slain.
Enter CADE and the rest*

CADE. Where's Dick, the butcher of Ashford?
DICK. Here, sir.
CADE. They fell before thee like sheep and oxen, and thou
behavedst
 thyself as if thou hadst been in thine own slaughter-house;
 therefore thus will I reward thee- the Lent shall be as long
 again as it is, and thou shalt have a licence to kill for a
 hundred lacking one.
DICK. I desire no more.
CADE. And, to speak truth, thou deserv'st no less. [Putting on SIR
 HUMPHREY'S brigandine] This monument of the victory will I
bear,
 and the bodies shall be dragged at my horse heels till I do come
 to London, where we will have the mayor's sword borne before us.
DICK. If we mean to thrive and do good, break open the gaols and
 let out the prisoners.
CADE. Fear not that, I warrant thee. Come, let's march towards
 London. *Exeunt*

SCENE IV. *London. The palace*

*Enter the KING with a supplication, and the QUEEN with
SUFFOLK'S head; the DUKE OF BUCKINGHAM, and the LORD
SAY*

QUEEN. Oft have I heard that grief softens the mind
 And makes it fearful and degenerate;
 Think therefore on revenge and cease to weep.
 But who can cease to weep, and look on this?
 Here may his head lie on my throbbing breast;

But where's the body that I should embrace?
BUCKINGHAM. What answer makes your Grace to the rebels'
  supplication?
KING HENRY. I'll send some holy bishop to entreat;
  For God forbid so many simple souls
  Should perish by the sword! And I myself,
  Rather than bloody war shall cut them short,
  Will parley with Jack Cade their general.
  But stay, I'll read it over once again.
QUEEN. Ah, barbarous villains! Hath this lovely face
  Rul'd like a wandering planet over me,
  And could it not enforce them to relent
  That were unworthy to behold the same?
KING HENRY. Lord Say, Jack Cade hath sworn to have thy head.
SAY. Ay, but I hope your Highness shall have his.
KING HENRY. How now, madam!
  Still lamenting and mourning for Suffolk's death?
  I fear me, love, if that I had been dead,
  Thou wouldst not have mourn'd so much for me.
QUEEN. No, my love, I should not mourn, but die for thee.

Enter A MESSENGER

KING HENRY. How now! What news? Why com'st thou in such
haste?
  MESSENGER. The rebels are in Southwark; fly, my lord!
  Jack Cade proclaims himself Lord Mortimer,
  Descended from the Duke of Clarence' house,
  And calls your Grace usurper, openly,
  And vows to crown himself in Westminster.
  His army is a ragged multitude
  Of hinds and peasants, rude and merciless;
  Sir Humphrey Stafford and his brother's death
  Hath given them heart and courage to proceed.
  All scholars, lawyers, courtiers, gentlemen,
  They call false caterpillars and intend their death.
KING HENRY. O graceless men! they know not what they do.
BUCKINGHAM. My gracious lord, retire to Killingworth
  Until a power be rais'd to put them down.

QUEEN. Ah, were the Duke of Suffolk now alive,
  These Kentish rebels would be soon appeas'd!
KING HENRY. Lord Say, the traitors hate thee;
  Therefore away with us to Killingworth.
SAY. So might your Grace's person be in danger.
  The sight of me is odious in their eyes;
  And therefore in this city will I stay
  And live alone as secret as I may.

Enter another MESSENGER

SECOND MESSENGER. Jack Cade hath gotten London Bridge.
  The citizens fly and forsake their houses;
  The rascal people, thirsting after prey,
  Join with the traitor; and they jointly swear
  To spoil the city and your royal court.
BUCKINGHAM. Then linger not, my lord; away, take horse.
KING HENRY. Come Margaret; God, our hope, will succour us.
QUEEN. My hope is gone, now Suffolk is deceas'd.
KING HENRY. [To LORD SAY] Farewell, my lord, trust not the Kentish
  rebels.
BUCKINGHAM. Trust nobody, for fear you be betray'd.
SAY. The trust I have is in mine innocence,
  And therefore am I bold and resolute. Exeunt

SCENE V. London. The Tower

Enter LORD SCALES Upon the Tower, walking. Then enter two or
three CITIZENS, below

SCALES. How now! Is Jack Cade slain?
FIRST CITIZEN. No, my lord, nor likely to be slain; for they have
  won the bridge, killing all those that withstand them.
  The Lord Mayor craves aid of your honour from the
  Tower, to defend the city from the rebels.

SCALES. Such aid as I can spare you shall command,
But I am troubled here with them myself;
The rebels have assay'd to win the Tower.
But get you to Smithfield, and gather head,
And thither I will send you Matthew Goffe;
Fight for your King, your country, and your lives;
And so, farewell, for I must hence again. Exeunt

SCENE VI. *London. Cannon street*

Enter JACK CADE and the rest, and strikes his staff on London Stone

CADE. Now is Mortimer lord of this city. And here, sitting upon London Stone, I charge and command that, of the city's cost, the pissing conduit run nothing but claret wine this first year of our reign. And now henceforward it shall be treason for any that calls me other than Lord Mortimer.

Enter a SOLDIER, running

SOLDIER. Jack Cade! Jack Cade!
CADE. Knock him down there. [They kill him]
SMITH. If this fellow be wise, he'll never call ye Jack Cade more; I think he hath a very fair warning.
DICK. My lord, there's an army gathered together in Smithfield.
CADE. Come then, let's go fight with them. But first go and set London Bridge on fire; and, if you can, burn down the Tower too. Come, let's away. Exeunt

SCENE VII. *London. Smithfield*

Alarums. MATTHEW GOFFE is slain, and all the rest. Then enter
JACK CADE, with his company

CADE. So, sirs. Now go some and pull down the Savoy; others to
th'
  Inns of Court; down with them all.
DICK. I have a suit unto your lordship.
CADE. Be it a lordship, thou shalt have it for that word.
DICK. Only that the laws of England may come out of your mouth.
JOHN. [Aside] Mass, 'twill be sore law then; for he was thrust in
  the mouth with a spear, and 'tis not whole yet.
SMITH. [Aside] Nay, John, it will be stinking law; for his breath
  stinks with eating toasted cheese.
CADE. I have thought upon it; it shall be so. Away, burn all the
  records of the realm. My mouth shall be the Parliament of
  England.
JOHN. [Aside] Then we are like to have biting statutes, unless his
  teeth be pull'd out.
CADE. And henceforward all things shall be in common.

Enter a MESSENGER

MESSENGER. My lord, a prize, a prize! Here's the Lord Say,
  which sold the towns in France; he that made us pay one and
  twenty fifteens, and one shining to the pound, the last subsidy.

Enter GEORGE BEVIS, with the LORD SAY

CADE. Well, he shall be beheaded for it ten times. Ah, thou say,
  thou serge, nay, thou buckram lord! Now art thou within point
  blank of our jurisdiction regal. What canst thou answer to my
  Majesty for giving up of Normandy unto Mounsieur Basimecu the
  Dauphin of France? Be it known unto thee by these presence, even
  the presence of Lord Mortimer, that I am the besom that must
  sweep the court clean of such filth as thou art. Thou hast most
  traitorously corrupted the youth of the realm in erecting a
  grammar school; and whereas, before, our forefathers had no other
  books but the score and the tally, thou hast caused printing to
  be us'd, and, contrary to the King, his crown, and dignity, thou
  hast built a paper-mill. It will be proved to thy face that thou

hast men about thee that usually talk of a noun and a verb, and such abominable words as no Christian ear can endure to hear. Thou hast appointed justices of peace, to call poor men before them about matters they were not able to answer. Moreover, thou hast put them in prison, and because they could not read, thou hast hang'd them, when, indeed, only for that cause they have been most worthy to live. Thou dost ride in a foot-cloth, dost thou not?

SAY. What of that?

CADE. Marry, thou ought'st not to let thy horse wear a cloak, when honester men than thou go in their hose and doublets.

DICK. And work in their shirt too, as myself, for example, that am a butcher.

SAY. You men of Kent-

DICK. What say you of Kent?

SAY. Nothing but this: 'tis 'bona terra, mala gens.'

CADE. Away with him, away with him! He speaks Latin.

SAY. Hear me but speak, and bear me where you will.
  Kent, in the Commentaries Caesar writ,
  Is term'd the civil'st place of all this isle.
  Sweet is the country, because full of riches;
  The people liberal valiant, active, wealthy;
  Which makes me hope you are not void of pity.
  I sold not Maine, I lost not Normandy;
  Yet, to recover them, would lose my life.
  Justice with favour have I always done;
  Pray'rs and tears have mov'd me, gifts could never.
  When have I aught exacted at your hands,
  But to maintain the King, the realm, and you?
  Large gifts have I bestow'd on learned clerks,
  Because my book preferr'd me to the King,
  And seeing ignorance is the curse of God,
  Knowledge the wing wherewith we fly to heaven,
  Unless you be possess'd with devilish spirits
  You cannot but forbear to murder me.
  This tongue hath parley'd unto foreign kings
  For your behoof.

CADE. Tut, when struck'st thou one blow in the field?

SAY. Great men have reaching hands. Oft have I struck

Those that I never saw, and struck them dead.

GEORGE. O monstrous coward! What, to come behind folks?

SAY. These cheeks are pale for watching for your good.

CADE. Give him a box o' th' ear, and that will make 'em red again.

SAY. Long sitting to determine poor men's causes
Hath made me full of sickness and diseases.

CADE. Ye shall have a hempen caudle then, and the help of hatchet.

DICK. Why dost thou quiver, man?

SAY. The palsy, and not fear, provokes me.

CADE. Nay, he nods at us, as who should say 'I'll be even with
you'; I'll see if his head will stand steadier on a pole, or no.
Take him away, and behead him.

SAY. Tell me: wherein have I offended most?
Have I affected wealth or honour? Speak.
Are my chests fill'd up with extorted gold?
Is my apparel sumptuous to behold?
Whom have I injur'd, that ye seek my death?
These hands are free from guiltless bloodshedding,
This breast from harbouring foul deceitful thoughts.
O, let me live!

CADE. [Aside] I feel remorse in myself with his words; but I'll
bridle it. He shall die, an it be but for pleading so well for
his life.- Away with him! He has a familiar under his tongue; he
speaks not o' God's name. Go, take him away, I say, and strike
off his head presently, and then break into his son-in-law's
house, Sir James Cromer, and strike off his head, and bring them
both upon two poles hither.

ALL. It shall be done.

SAY. Ah, countrymen! if when you make your pray'rs,
God should be so obdurate as yourselves,
How would it fare with your departed souls?
And therefore yet relent and save my life.

CADE. Away with him, and do as I command ye. [Exeunt some with
LORD SAY] The proudest peer in the realm shall not wear a head
on his shoulders, unless he pay me tribute; there shall not a
maid be married, but she shall pay to me her maidenhead ere they
have it. Men shall hold of me in capite; and we charge and

81

command that their wives be as free as heart can wish or tongue can tell.

DICK. My lord, when shall we go to Cheapside, and take up commodities upon our bills?

CADE. Marry, presently.

ALL. O, brave!

Re-enter one with the heads

CADE. But is not this braver? Let them kiss one another, for they lov'd well when they were alive. Now part them again, lest they consult about the giving up of some more towns in France. Soldiers, defer the spoil of the city until night; for with these borne before us instead of maces will we ride through the streets, and at every corner have them kiss. Away! Exeunt

SCENE VIII. Southwark

Alarum and retreat. Enter again CADE and all his rabblement

CADE. Up Fish Street! down Saint Magnus' Corner! Kill and knock down! Throw them into Thames! [Sound a parley] What noise is this I hear? Dare any be so bold to sound retreat or parley when I command them kill?

Enter BUCKINGHAM and old CLIFFORD, attended

BUCKINGHAM. Ay, here they be that dare and will disturb thee.
And therefore yet relent, and save my life.
Know, Cade, we come ambassadors from the King
Unto the commons whom thou hast misled;
And here pronounce free pardon to them all
That will forsake thee and go home in peace.
CLIFFORD. What say ye, countrymen? Will ye relent
And yield to mercy whilst 'tis offer'd you,
Or let a rebel lead you to your deaths?

Who loves the King, and will embrace his pardon,
Fling up his cap and say 'God save his Majesty!'
Who hateth him and honours not his father,
Henry the Fifth, that made all France to quake,
Shake he his weapon at us and pass by.
ALL. God save the King! God save the King!
CADE. What, Buckingham and Clifford, are ye so brave?
And you, base peasants, do ye believe him? Will you needs be
hang'd with your about your necks? Hath my sword therefore
broke
through London gates, that you should leave me at the White Hart
in Southwark? I thought ye would never have given out these
arms
till you had recovered your ancient freedom. But you are all
recreants and dastards, and delight to live in slavery to the
nobility. Let them break your backs with burdens, take your
houses over your heads, ravish your wives and daughters before
your faces. For me, I will make shift for one; and so God's curse
light upon you all!
ALL. We'll follow Cade, we'll follow Cade!
CLIFFORD. Is Cade the son of Henry the Fifth,
That thus you do exclaim you'll go with him?
Will he conduct you through the heart of France,
And make the meanest of you earls and dukes?
Alas, he hath no home, no place to fly to;
Nor knows he how to live but by the spoil,
Unless by robbing of your friends and us.
Were't not a shame that whilst you live at jar
The fearful French, whom you late vanquished,
Should make a start o'er seas and vanquish you?
Methinks already in this civil broil
I see them lording it in London streets,
Crying 'Villiago!' unto all they meet.
Better ten thousand base-born Cades miscarry
Than you should stoop unto a Frenchman's mercy.
To France, to France, and get what you have lost;
Spare England, for it is your native coast.
Henry hath money; you are strong and manly.
God on our side, doubt not of victory.

ALL. A Clifford! a Clifford! We'll follow the King and Clifford.

CADE. Was ever feather so lightly blown to and fro as this
   multitude? The name of Henry the Fifth hales them to an hundred
   mischiefs, and makes them leave me desolate. I see them lay their
   heads together to surprise me. My sword make way for me for
here
   is no staying. In despite of the devils and hell, have through
   the very middest of you! and heavens and honour be witness that
   no want of resolution in me, but only my followers' base and
   ignominious treasons, makes me betake me to my heels.
Exit

BUCKINGHAM. What, is he fled? Go some, and follow him;
   And he that brings his head unto the King
   Shall have a thousand crowns for his reward.
                         Exeunt some of them
   Follow me, soldiers; we'll devise a mean
   To reconcile you all unto the King. Exeunt

SCENE IX. *Killing, worth Castle*

Sound trumpets. Enter KING, QUEEN, and SOMERSET, on the
terrace

KING HENRY. Was ever king that joy'd an earthly throne
   And could command no more content than I?
   No sooner was I crept out of my cradle
   But I was made a king, at nine months old.
   Was never subject long'd to be a King
   As I do long and wish to be a subject.

Enter BUCKINGHAM and old CLIFFORD

BUCKINGHAM. Health and glad tidings to your Majesty!
KING HENRY. Why, Buckingham, is the traitor Cade surpris'd?
   Or is he but retir'd to make him strong?

Enter, below, multitudes, with halters about their necks

CLIFFORD. He is fled, my lord, and all his powers do yield,
  And humbly thus, with halters on their necks,
  Expect your Highness' doom of life or death.
KING HENRY. Then, heaven, set ope thy everlasting gates,
  To entertain my vows of thanks and praise!
  Soldiers, this day have you redeem'd your lives,
  And show'd how well you love your Prince and country.
  Continue still in this so good a mind,
  And Henry, though he be infortunate,
  Assure yourselves, will never be unkind.
  And so, with thanks and pardon to you all,
  I do dismiss you to your several countries.
ALL. God save the King! God save the King!

Enter a MESSENGER

MESSENGER. Please it your Grace to be advertised
  The Duke of York is newly come from Ireland
  And with a puissant and a mighty power
  Of gallowglasses and stout kerns
  Is marching hitherward in proud array,
  And still proclaimeth, as he comes along,
  His arms are only to remove from thee
  The Duke of Somerset, whom he terms a traitor.
KING HENRY. Thus stands my state, 'twixt Cade and York distress'd;
  Like to a ship that, having scap'd a tempest,
  Is straightway calm'd, and boarded with a pirate;
  But now is Cade driven back, his men dispers'd,
  And now is York in arms to second him.
  I pray thee, Buckingham, go and meet him
  And ask him what's the reason of these arms.
  Tell him I'll send Duke Edmund to the Tower-
  And Somerset, we will commit thee thither
  Until his army be dismiss'd from him.
SOMERSET. My lord,
  I'll yield myself to prison willingly,

Or unto death, to do my country good.

KING HENRY. In any case be not too rough in terms,
  For he is fierce and cannot brook hard language.

BUCKINGHAM. I will, my lord, and doubt not so to deal
  As all things shall redound unto your good.

KING HENRY. Come, wife, let's in, and learn to govern better;
  For yet may England curse my wretched reign.

                            Flourish. Exeunt

SCENE X. Kent. Iden's garden

Enter CADE

CADE. Fie on ambitions! Fie on myself, that have a sword and
yet am ready to famish! These five days have I hid me in these
woods and durst not peep out, for all the country is laid for me;
but now am I so hungry that, if I might have a lease of my life
for a thousand years, I could stay no longer. Wherefore, on a
brick wall have I climb'd into this garden, to see if I can eat
grass or pick a sallet another while, which is not amiss to cool a
man's stomach this hot weather. And I think this word 'sallet'
was born to do me good; for many a time, but for a sallet, my
brain-pain had been cleft with a brown bill; and many a time,
when I have been dry, and bravely marching, it hath serv'd me
instead of a quart-pot to drink in; and now the word 'sallet' must
serve me to feed on.

Enter IDEN

IDEN. Lord, who would live turmoiled in the court
  And may enjoy such quiet walks as these?
  This small inheritance my father left me
  Contenteth me, and worth a monarchy.
  I seek not to wax great by others' waning
  Or gather wealth I care not with what envy;
  Sufficeth that I have maintains my state,

86

And sends the poor well pleased from my gate.

CADE. Here's the lord of the soil come to seize me for a stray, for
    entering his fee-simple without leave. Ah, villain, thou wilt
    betray me, and get a thousand crowns of the King by carrying my
    head to him; but I'll make thee eat iron like an ostrich and
    swallow my sword like a great pin ere thou and I part.

IDEN. Why, rude companion, whatsoe'er thou be,
    I know thee not; why then should I betray thee?
    Is't not enough to break into my garden
    And like a thief to come to rob my grounds,
    Climbing my walls in spite of me the owner,
    But thou wilt brave me with these saucy terms?

CADE. Brave thee? Ay, by the best blood that ever was broach'd,
and
    beard thee too. Look on me well: I have eat no meat these five
    days, yet come thou and thy five men and if I do not leave you
    all as dead as a door-nail, I pray God I may never eat grass
    more.

IDEN. Nay, it shall ne'er be said, while England stands,
    That Alexander Iden, an esquire of Kent,
    Took odds to combat a poor famish'd man.
    Oppose thy steadfast-gazing eyes to mine;
    See if thou canst outface me with thy looks;
    Set limb to limb, and thou art far the lesser;
    Thy hand is but a finger to my fist,
    Thy leg a stick compared with this truncheon;
    My foot shall fight with all the strength thou hast,
    And if mine arm be heaved in the air,
    Thy grave is digg'd already in the earth.
    As for words, whose greatness answers words,
    Let this my sword report what speech forbears.

CADE. By my valour, the most complete champion that ever I
heard!
    Steel, if thou turn the edge, or cut not out the burly bon'd
    clown in chines of beef ere thou sleep in thy sheath, I beseech
    God on my knees thou mayst be turn'd to hobnails. [Here they
    fight; CADE falls] O, I am slain! famine and no other hath slain
    me. Let ten thousand devils come against me, and give me but the
    ten meals I have lost, and I'd defy them all. Wither, garden, and

87

be henceforth a burying place to all that do dwell in this house, because the unconquered soul of Cade is fled.

IDEN. Is't Cade that I have slain, that monstrous traitor?
Sword, I will hallow thee for this thy deed
And hang thee o'er my tomb when I am dead.
Ne'er shall this blood be wiped from thy point,
But thou shalt wear it as a herald's coat
To emblaze the honour that thy master got.

CADE. Iden, farewell; and be proud of thy victory. Tell Kent from me she hath lost her best man, and exhort all the world to be cowards; for I, that never feared any, am vanquished by famine, not by valour. [Dies]

IDEN. How much thou wrong'st me, heaven be my judge.
Die, damned wretch, the curse of her that bare thee!
And as I thrust thy body in with my sword,
So wish I, I might thrust thy soul to hell.
Hence will I drag thee headlong by the heels
Unto a dunghill, which shall be thy grave,
And there cut off thy most ungracious head,
Which I will bear in triumph to the King,
Leaving thy trunk for crows to feed upon. Exit

ACT V. SCENE I. Fields between Dartford and Blackheath

Enter YORK, and his army of Irish, with drum and colours

YORK. From Ireland thus comes York to claim his right
And pluck the crown from feeble Henry's head:
Ring bells aloud, burn bonfires clear and bright,
To entertain great England's lawful king.
Ah, sancta majestas! who would not buy thee dear?
Let them obey that knows not how to rule;
This hand was made to handle nought but gold.
I cannot give due action to my words
Except a sword or sceptre balance it.
A sceptre shall it have, have I a soul
On which I'll toss the flower-de-luce of France.

Enter BUCKINGHAM

    [Aside] Whom have we here? Buckingham, to disturb me?
    The King hath sent him, sure: I must dissemble.
BUCKINGHAM. York, if thou meanest well I greet thee well.
YORK. Humphrey of Buckingham, I accept thy greeting.
    Art thou a messenger, or come of pleasure?
BUCKINGHAM. A messenger from Henry, our dread liege,
    To know the reason of these arms in peace;
    Or why thou, being a subject as I am,
    Against thy oath and true allegiance sworn,
    Should raise so great a power without his leave,
    Or dare to bring thy force so near the court.
YORK. [Aside] Scarce can I speak, my choler is so great.
    O, I could hew up rocks and fight with flint,
    I am so angry at these abject terms;
    And now, like Ajax Telamonius,
    On sheep or oxen could I spend my fury.
    I am far better born than is the King,
    More like a king, more kingly in my thoughts;
    But I must make fair weather yet awhile,
    Till Henry be more weak and I more strong.-
    Buckingham, I prithee, pardon me
    That I have given no answer all this while;
    My mind was troubled with deep melancholy.
    The cause why I have brought this army hither
    Is to remove proud Somerset from the King,
    Seditious to his Grace and to the state.
BUCKINGHAM. That is too much presumption on thy part;
    But if thy arms be to no other end,
    The King hath yielded unto thy demand:
    The Duke of Somerset is in the Tower.
YORK. Upon thine honour, is he prisoner?
BUCKINGHAM. Upon mine honour, he is prisoner.
YORK. Then, Buckingham, I do dismiss my pow'rs.
    Soldiers, I thank you all; disperse yourselves;
    Meet me to-morrow in Saint George's field,
    You shall have pay and everything you wish.
    And let my sovereign, virtuous Henry,

Command my eldest son, nay, all my sons,
As pledges of my fealty and love.
I'll send them all as willing as I live:
Lands, goods, horse, armour, anything I have,
Is his to use, so Somerset may die.
BUCKINGHAM. York, I commend this kind submission.
We twain will go into his Highness' tent.

Enter the KING, and attendants

KING HENRY. Buckingham, doth York intend no harm to us,
That thus he marcheth with thee arm in arm?
YORK. In all submission and humility
York doth present himself unto your Highness.
KING HENRY. Then what intends these forces thou dost bring?
YORK. To heave the traitor Somerset from hence,
And fight against that monstrous rebel Cade,
Who since I heard to be discomfited.

Enter IDEN, with CADE's head

IDEN. If one so rude and of so mean condition
May pass into the presence of a king,
Lo, I present your Grace a traitor's head,
The head of Cade, whom I in combat slew.
KING HENRY. The head of Cade! Great God, how just art Thou!
O, let me view his visage, being dead,
That living wrought me such exceeding trouble.
Tell me, my friend, art thou the man that slew him?
IDEN. I was, an't like your Majesty.
KING HENRY. How art thou call'd? And what is thy degree?
IDEN. Alexander Iden, that's my name;
A poor esquire of Kent that loves his king.
BUCKINGHAM. So please it you, my lord, 'twere not amiss
He were created knight for his good service.
KING HENRY. Iden, kneel down. [He kneels] Rise up a knight.
We give thee for reward a thousand marks,
And will that thou thenceforth attend on us.
IDEN. May Iden live to merit such a bounty,
And never live but true unto his liege!

Enter the QUEEN and SOMERSET

KING HENRY. See, Buckingham! Somerset comes with th'
Queen:
  Go, bid her hide him quickly from the Duke.
QUEEN. For thousand Yorks he shall not hide his head,
  But boldly stand and front him to his face.
YORK. How now! Is Somerset at liberty?
  Then, York, unloose thy long-imprisoned thoughts
  And let thy tongue be equal with thy heart.
  Shall I endure the sight of Somerset?
  False king, why hast thou broken faith with me,
  Knowing how hardly I can brook abuse?
  King did I call thee? No, thou art not king;
  Not fit to govern and rule multitudes,
  Which dar'st not, no, nor canst not rule a traitor.
  That head of thine doth not become a crown;
  Thy hand is made to grasp a palmer's staff,
  And not to grace an awful princely sceptre.
  That gold must round engirt these brows of mine,
  Whose smile and frown, like to Achilles' spear,
  Is able with the change to kill and cure.
  Here is a hand to hold a sceptre up,
  And with the same to act controlling laws.
  Give place. By heaven, thou shalt rule no more
  O'er him whom heaven created for thy ruler.
SOMERSET. O monstrous traitor! I arrest thee, York,
  Of capital treason 'gainst the King and crown.
  Obey, audacious traitor; kneel for grace.
YORK. Wouldst have me kneel? First let me ask of these,
  If they can brook I bow a knee to man.
  Sirrah, call in my sons to be my bail: Exit attendant
  I know, ere thy will have me go to ward,
  They'll pawn their swords for my enfranchisement.
QUEEN. Call hither Clifford; bid him come amain,
  To say if that the bastard boys of York
  Shall be the surety for their traitor father.
                         Exit BUCKINGHAM
YORK. O blood-bespotted Neapolitan,

Outcast of Naples, England's bloody scourge!
The sons of York, thy betters in their birth,
Shall be their father's bail; and bane to those
That for my surety will refuse the boys!

Enter EDWARD and RICHARD PLANTAGENET

See where they come: I'll warrant they'll make it good.

Enter CLIFFORD and his SON

QUEEN. And here comes Clifford to deny their bail.
CLIFFORD. Health and all happiness to my lord the King!
                              [Kneels]
YORK. I thank thee, Clifford. Say, what news with thee?
  Nay, do not fright us with an angry look.
  We are thy sovereign, Clifford, kneel again;
  For thy mistaking so, we pardon thee.
CLIFFORD. This is my King, York, I do not mistake;
  But thou mistakes me much to think I do.
  To Bedlam with him! Is the man grown mad?
KING HENRY. Ay, Clifford; a bedlam and ambitious humour
  Makes him oppose himself against his king.
CLIFFORD. He is a traitor; let him to the Tower,
  And chop away that factious pate of his.
QUEEN. He is arrested, but will not obey;
  His sons, he says, shall give their words for him.
YORK. Will you not, sons?
EDWARD. Ay, noble father, if our words will serve.
RICHARD. And if words will not, then our weapons shall.
CLIFFORD. Why, what a brood of traitors have we here!
YORK. Look in a glass, and call thy image so:
  I am thy king, and thou a false-heart traitor.
  Call hither to the stake my two brave bears,
  That with the very shaking of their chains
  They may astonish these fell-lurking curs.
  Bid Salisbury and Warwick come to me.

Enter the EARLS OF WARWICK and SALISBURY

CLIFFORD. Are these thy bears? We'll bait thy bears to death,
  And manacle the berard in their chains,
  If thou dar'st bring them to the baiting-place.
RICHARD. Oft have I seen a hot o'er weening cur
  Run back and bite, because he was withheld;
  Who, being suffer'd, with the bear's fell paw,
  Hath clapp'd his tail between his legs and cried;
  And such a piece of service will you do,
  If you oppose yourselves to match Lord Warwick.
CLIFFORD. Hence, heap of wrath, foul indigested lump,
  As crooked in thy manners as thy shape!
YORK. Nay, we shall heat you thoroughly anon.
CLIFFORD. Take heed, lest by your heat you burn yourselves.
KING HENRY. Why, Warwick, hath thy knee forgot to bow?
  Old Salisbury, shame to thy silver hair,
  Thou mad misleader of thy brainsick son!
  What, wilt thou on thy death-bed play the ruffian
  And seek for sorrow with thy spectacles?
  O, where is faith? O, where is loyalty?
  If it be banish'd from the frosty head,
  Where shall it find a harbour in the earth?
  Wilt thou go dig a grave to find out war
  And shame thine honourable age with blood?
  Why art thou old, and want'st experience?
  Or wherefore dost abuse it, if thou hast it?
  For shame! In duty bend thy knee to me,
  That bows unto the grave with mickle age.
SALISBURY. My lord, I have considered with myself
  The tide of this most renowned duke,
  And in my conscience do repute his Grace
  The rightful heir to England's royal seat.
KING HENRY. Hast thou not sworn allegiance unto me?
SALISBURY. I have.
KING HENRY. Canst thou dispense with heaven for such an oath?
SALISBURY. It is great sin to swear unto a sin;
  But greater sin to keep a sinful oath.
  Who can be bound by any solemn vow
  To do a murd'rous deed, to rob a man,
  To force a spotless virgin's chastity,

To reave the orphan of his patrimony,
To wring the widow from her custom'd right,
And have no other reason for this wrong
But that he was bound by a solemn oath?

QUEEN. A subtle traitor needs no sophister.

KING HENRY. Call Buckingham, and bid him arm himself.

YORK. Call Buckingham, and all the friends thou hast,
I am resolv'd for death or dignity.

CLIFFORD. The first I warrant thee, if dreams prove true.

WARWICK. You were best to go to bed and dream again
To keep thee from the tempest of the field.

CLIFFORD. I am resolv'd to bear a greater storm
Than any thou canst conjure up to-day;
And that I'll write upon thy burgonet,
Might I but know thee by thy household badge.

WARWICK. Now, by my father's badge, old Nevil's crest,
The rampant bear chain'd to the ragged staff,
This day I'll wear aloft my burgonet,
As on a mountain-top the cedar shows,
That keeps his leaves in spite of any storm,
Even to affright thee with the view thereof.

CLIFFORD. And from thy burgonet I'll rend thy bear
And tread it under foot with all contempt,
Despite the berard that protects the bear.

YOUNG CLIFFORD. And so to arms, victorious father,
To quell the rebels and their complices.

RICHARD. Fie! charity, for shame! Speak not in spite,
For you shall sup with Jesu Christ to-night.

YOUNG CLIFFORD. Foul stigmatic, that's more than thou canst
tell.

RICHARD. If not in heaven, you'll surely sup in hell.

Exeunt severally

SCENE II. Saint Albans

Alarums to the battle. Enter WARWICK

WARWICK. Clifford of Cumberland, 'tis Warwick calls;
  And if thou dost not hide thee from the bear,
  Now, when the angry trumpet sounds alarum
  And dead men's cries do fill the empty air,
  Clifford, I say, come forth and fight with me.
  Proud northern lord, Clifford of Cumberland,
  WARWICK is hoarse with calling thee to arms.

Enter YORK

How now, my noble lord! what, all a-foot?
YORK. The deadly-handed Clifford slew my steed;
  But match to match I have encount'red him,
  And made a prey for carrion kites and crows
  Even of the bonny beast he lov'd so well.

Enter OLD CLIFFORD

WARWICK. Of one or both of us the time is come.
YORK. Hold, Warwick, seek thee out some other chase,
  For I myself must hunt this deer to death.
WARWICK. Then, nobly, York; 'tis for a crown thou fight'st.
  As I intend, Clifford, to thrive to-day,
  It grieves my soul to leave thee unassail'd. Exit
CLIFFORD. What seest thou in me, York? Why dost thou pause?
YORK. With thy brave bearing should I be in love
  But that thou art so fast mine enemy.
CLIFFORD. Nor should thy prowess want praise and esteem
  But that 'tis shown ignobly and in treason.
YORK. So let it help me now against thy sword,
  As I in justice and true right express it!
CLIFFORD. My soul and body on the action both!
YORK. A dreadful lay! Address thee instantly.
                    [They fight and CLIFFORD falls]
CLIFFORD. La fin couronne les oeuvres. [Dies]
YORK. Thus war hath given thee peace, for thou art still.
  Peace with his soul, heaven, if it be thy will! Exit

Enter YOUNG CLIFFORD

  YOUNG CLIFFORD. Shame and confusion! All is on the rout;
   Fear frames disorder, and disorder wounds
   Where it should guard. O war, thou son of hell,
   Whom angry heavens do make their minister,
   Throw in the frozen bosoms of our part
   Hot coals of vengeance! Let no soldier fly.
   He that is truly dedicate to war
   Hath no self-love; nor he that loves himself
   Hath not essentially, but by circumstance,
   The name of valour. [Sees his father's body]
   O, let the vile world end
   And the premised flames of the last day
   Knit earth and heaven together!
   Now let the general trumpet blow his blast,
   Particularities and petty sounds
   To cease! Wast thou ordain'd, dear father,
   To lose thy youth in peace and to achieve
   The silver livery of advised age,
   And in thy reverence and thy chair-days thus
   To die in ruffian battle? Even at this sight
   My heart is turn'd to stone; and while 'tis mine
   It shall be stony. York not our old men spares;
   No more will I their babes. Tears virginal
   Shall be to me even as the dew to fire;
   And beauty, that the tyrant oft reclaims,
   Shall to my flaming wrath be oil and flax.
   Henceforth I will not have to do with pity:
   Meet I an infant of the house of York,
   Into as many gobbets will I cut it
   As wild Medea young Absyrtus did;
   In cruelty will I seek out my fame.
   Come, thou new ruin of old Clifford's house;
   As did Aeneas old Anchises bear,
   So bear I thee upon my manly shoulders;
   But then Aeneas bare a living load,
   Nothing so heavy as these woes of mine.
                        Exit with the body

Enter RICHARD and SOMERSET to fight. SOMERSET is killed

RICHARD. So, lie thou there;
  For underneath an alehouse' paltry sign,
  The Castle in Saint Albans, Somerset
  Hath made the wizard famous in his death.
  Sword, hold thy temper; heart, be wrathful still:
  Priests pray for enemies, but princes kill. Exit

Fight. Excursions. Enter KING, QUEEN, and others

QUEEN. Away, my lord! You are slow; for shame, away!
KING HENRY. Can we outrun the heavens? Good Margaret, stay.
QUEEN. What are you made of? You'll nor fight nor fly.
  Now is it manhood, wisdom, and defence,
  To give the enemy way, and to secure us
  By what we can, which can no more but fly.
                 [Alarum afar off]
  If you be ta'en, we then should see the bottom
  Of all our fortunes; but if we haply scape-
  As well we may, if not through your neglect-
  We shall to London get, where you are lov'd,
  And where this breach now in our fortunes made
  May readily be stopp'd.

Re-enter YOUNG CLIFFORD

YOUNG CLIFFORD. But that my heart's on future mischief set,
  I would speak blasphemy ere bid you fly;
  But fly you must; uncurable discomfit
  Reigns in the hearts of all our present parts.
  Away, for your relief! and we will live
  To see their day and them our fortune give.
  Away, my lord, away! Exeunt

SCENE III. Fields near Saint Albans

Alarum. Retreat. Enter YORK, RICHARD, WARWICK, and soldiers, with drum and colours

YORK. Of Salisbury, who can report of him,
  That winter lion, who in rage forgets
  Aged contusions and all brush of time
  And, like a gallant in the brow of youth,
  Repairs him with occasion? This happy day
  Is not itself, nor have we won one foot,
  If Salisbury be lost.
RICHARD. My noble father,
  Three times to-day I holp him to his horse,
  Three times bestrid him, thrice I led him off,
  Persuaded him from any further act;
  But still where danger was, still there I met him;
  And like rich hangings in a homely house,
  So was his will in his old feeble body.
  But, noble as he is, look where he comes.

Enter SALISBURY

SALISBURY. Now, by my sword, well hast thou fought to-day!
  By th' mass, so did we all. I thank you, Richard:
  God knows how long it is I have to live,
  And it hath pleas'd Him that three times to-day
  You have defended me from imminent death.
  Well, lords, we have not got that which we have;
  'Tis not enough our foes are this time fled,
  Being opposites of such repairing nature.
YORK. I know our safety is to follow them;
  For, as I hear, the King is fled to London
  To call a present court of Parliament.
  Let us pursue him ere the writs go forth.
  What says Lord Warwick? Shall we after them?
WARWICK. After them? Nay, before them, if we can.
  Now, by my faith, lords, 'twas a glorious day:
  Saint Albans' battle, won by famous York,
  Shall be eterniz'd in all age to come.

Sound drum and trumpets and to London all;
And more such days as these to us befall!

Exeunt

Printed in Great Britain
by Amazon

36278586R00057